BLACK CIVIL RIGHTS CHAMPIONS

BLACK CIVIL RIGHTS CHAMPIONS

Kimberly Hayes Taylor

The Oliver Press, Inc.
Minneapolis

The Oliver Press, Inc.
Charlotte Square
5707 West 36th Street
Minneapolis, MN 55416-2510

Library of Congress Cataloging-in-Publication Data

Taylor, Kimberly Hayes, 1962-
Black civil rights champions / Kimberly Hayes Taylor.
p.   cm. — (Profiles)
Includes bibliographical references (p.) and index.
ISBN 1-881508-22-6
1. Civil rights workers—United States—Biography—Juvenile literature. 2. Afro-Americans—Biography—Juvenile literature.
3. Afro-Americans—Civil rights—Juvenile literature. 4. Civil rights movements—United States—History—20th century—Juvenile literature. I. Title. II. Series: Profiles (Minneapolis, Minn.)
E185.96.T39 1995
323'.092'2—dc20
[B]   94-45652
                                                      CIP
                                                       AC

ISBN: 1-881508-22-6
Profiles XVII
Printed in the United States of America

99 98 97 96 95   8 7 6 5 4 3 2 1

Contents

"Freedom marchers" visited several southern cities during the 1960s to ensure that civil rights laws were being enforced.

Introduction

This book is about twentieth-century African Americans who fought for human rights and social justice even while the odds were against them. They worked hard because they wanted everyone in the United States to have the same rights and to be treated as equals. These civil rights champions knew that factors such as skin color, ancestry, and income should not affect someone's rights as a U.S. citizen.

All of the people profiled in this book were born after 1865, the year the Civil War ended and slavery became illegal in the United States. But racial discrimination and racially motivated violence have persisted throughout the 1900s, leading many Americans to continue to struggle for equality.

Many of the people in this book are no longer living, but their legacy continues to influence our society. Others are still living, and we have the opportunity to watch them work to make more changes in our society. As the United States continues to strive for true racial equality, all of us have the opportunity to join in the struggle for which some of these leaders gave their lives.

White and black people attended this 1873 convention that promoted equal rights for both races.

Martin Luther King Jr. (front row, left) and other civil rights activists held peaceful demonstrations to increase the opportunities for African Americans.

Martin Luther King Jr. is famous for his dream that all children, no matter their color, would walk together hand in hand. Malcolm X envisioned a time when African Americans would stand up for their rights without fear. He also believed that sometimes peaceful efforts alone would not be enough to accomplish his goals.

9

W.E.B. Du Bois proved that an African American could have a voice, even though it might not be a popular one. During the 1950s, Thurgood Marshall, attorney for the National Association for the Advancement of Colored People (NAACP), helped to win a landmark U.S. Supreme Court decision against racial segregation. Marshall later became the first African American to sit on that court.

From an early age, James Farmer decided he was not going to let anyone oppress him. As an adult, he became a leader of the Congress of Racial Equality (CORE), an important organization during the civil rights movement of the 1960s. NAACP field secretary Ella Baker helped show young people just how powerful they could be in the fight against racial discrimination. After spending several years as a civil rights activist, Andrew Young led fights in the U.S. political arena during the 1970s. He is one of the of most respected African Americans alive today.

Despite the gains that African Americans have made over the past few decades, racial imbalance still exists. Compared with whites, a lower percentage of African Americans graduate from high school, and fewer enroll in colleges. Many of them become so frustrated by everyday life at school and in their community that they give up and drop out in greater numbers than their white peers. Many do not receive the same kind of encouragement to continue their education as white students often do. For these reasons, many black students do not realize how much they can accomplish.

In the job market, African Americans still face discrimination. Sometimes they cannot get good jobs because some white-owned companies prefer to hire white job seekers. Then, when blacks are hired, they may find they are not paid as much as their white counterparts.

As a youth, civil rights leader Malcolm X had shown promise in his studies, but he quit school and landed in prison, where he read books voraciously.

11

Blacks today, however, seldom experience the kind of blatant racism they once faced in the past, when discriminatory "Jim Crow" laws legally prevented them from having the same opportunities as whites. And while society is still far from colorblind, it is important to remember that only a few decades ago young African-American men and women were being beaten for doing what they knew was right. The civil rights movement helped to end many discriminatory practices—and lynchings—but not the racism that led to injustice and violence against black people. By learning about the struggles that civil rights leaders have faced in the past, young people can find ways to make the United States a better place in the future.

From the mid-1800s into the first half of the 1900s, mobs of whites illegally hanged—or "lynched"— blacks who were accused, but often not convicted, of crimes. The term lynch may be derived from an eighteenth-century Virginia planter named Charles Lynch, who established an illegal "court" to punish suspected criminals.

Although sometimes criticized by his colleagues for trying to make reforms too quickly, W.E.B. Du Bois (1868-1963) believed African Americans deserved legal and social equality in the United States.

1

W.E.B. Du Bois
Founder of the NAACP

*W*illiam Edward Burghardt Du Bois was old-fashioned and stately in his ways and with his words—an approach that made him as many enemies as friends. During his lifetime, which spanned almost a century, Du Bois changed the way Americans—particularly African Americans—thought about themselves.

W.E.B. Du Bois was born on February 23, 1868, in Great Barrington, Massachusetts, to Alfred and Mary Silvina Du Bois. He was of African American, French, Dutch, and Native American ancestry, but he considered himself to be an African American. After graduating from high school in Great Barrington, where he had been the only black student, Du Bois attended Fisk University, a black college in Nashville, Tennessee.

W.E.B. Du Bois grew up during the Reconstruction period following the Civil War. Although slavery was now outlawed in every state, black people were still excluded from much of white society. Nevertheless, black people were strong within their own communities. By the late 1800s, blacks owned their own schools, churches, and newspapers. Black neighborhoods had their own

This photograph shows many black men at work in a phosphate mine in Florida during the 1890s. After the Civil War ended in 1865, many African Americans could only find jobs doing manual labor.

community aid societies, women's groups, banks, insurance companies, social clubs, and labor unions.

In 1895, Du Bois enrolled at Harvard University, where he earned a doctoral degree in social science. His dissertation, *The Suppression of the African Slave Trade*, was published in 1896. That same year, the U.S. Supreme Court ruling in *Plessy v. Ferguson* legitimized racial segregation. In *Plessy*, the Court ruled that Louisiana had the right to provide "separate but equal" railroad accommodations. This led to a system of segregation laws in the South. These "Jim Crow" laws, as they were called, would remain intact in the United States for the next 60 years.

In 1897, Du Bois became a professor of history at Atlanta University, a black college in Georgia, and taught there until 1910. While in Atlanta, he helped to start the American Negro Academy, America's first black "think tank" (a group organized to research and solve social or political problems). Du Bois also wrote *The Souls of Black Folks*, a compilation of his essays about the black experience. The book included his negative opinions about Booker T. Washington, a noted African-American leader and educator who was advising black people to accept segregation and learn marketable skills that would enable them to get a good job and contribute to society. To foster his beliefs, Washington had founded the Tuskegee Institute in Tuskegee, Alabama. This college trained thousands of black people in practical trades such as

Booker T. Washington (1856-1915) taught his students at the Tuskegee Institute self-respect and job skills that would make them financially secure in white society.

plumbing, carpentry, farming, blacksmithing, and mechanics. Washington felt that if blacks obtained economic independence, they would eventually be accepted by whites and allowed to live in peace.

Washington had become a popular lecturer and an authoritative voice throughout the nation. In 1896, he had become the first African American to receive an honorary doctorate degree from Harvard University. Whites tended to support Washington because of his opinion that blacks should remain separate but equal. When government leaders wanted to make political appointments, they asked Washington to recommend other African Americans to fill the positions.

Du Bois and other critics of Booker T. Washington believed that blacks would never be treated as equals if segregation continued. Du Bois pointed out that although the Civil War had ended slavery, many white Americans continued to beat and lynch blacks. Du Bois knew that changes had to be made. In his speeches and articles, he eloquently expressed the tension felt by black Americans. Washington's followers, on the other hand, thought Du Bois was too radical, sometimes calling him the "professor of hysterics."

Du Bois's vision was global. He wanted to uplift black people all over the world, but he felt the movement had to start in the United States. He told African Americans to be "inspired with the divine faith of our black mothers, that our blood and the dust of battle will march victorious, . . . a mighty nation, a peculiar people, to speak to the nations of the earth a divine truth that shall make them free." Unlike many of his contemporaries who used the Bible to preach against discrimination or to help give people hope for the future, Du Bois did not want to bring religion into the racial debate.

During the early 1900s, Du Bois directly confronted Booker T. Washington and his followers by publicly saying the following:

> As to Mr. Washington, the people who think I am one of those who oppose him, they are perfectly correct. I have no personal opinion of him—I honor much of his work. But his platform has done the race infinite harm, and I'm working against it with all my might.

The bitter relationship between Du Bois and Washington would have parallels among other African-American leaders, including the tension between abolitionist Frederick Douglass and accommodator Charles Lenox Redmon during the mid-1800s, and the opposing philosophies held by peacemaker Martin Luther King Jr. and the more militant Malcolm X during the 1960s.

Because black people made up only about ten percent of the U.S. population during the early 1900s, Du Bois realized they would not get much further in their pursuit of equality without white allies. Du Bois strongly supported the women's suffrage movement and said that no one with even one drop of African blood should oppose the suffragists working to give white women the right to vote. However, he conceded, there was "not the slightest reason for supposing that white American women . . . are going to be any more intellectual, liberal, or humane toward the black, the poor and unfortunate than white men are." While he had little faith that white women would let black people gain more rights—even if black people were willing to help them—Du Bois believed every effort to gain white support was worthwhile.

By the time he wrote a letter to several middle-class African-American professionals asking them to meet him in Niagara Falls in 1905 to start a new organization to attack racism, W.E.B. Du Bois had already built himself a reputation as an "agitator-prophet." In his letter, Du Bois had told the black leaders to come prepared to organize an aggressive plan of action for African-American freedom. "We claim for ourselves every single right that belongs to a freeborn American—political, civil, social; and until we get these rights we will never cease to protest and assail the ears of America. The battle we wage is not for ourselves but for all true Americans," he once said.

The Niagara Falls meeting convened in 1905 on the Canadian side of the falls because there were no segregated facilities where blacks could hold meetings on the U.S. side. Approximately 30 black leaders came to the meeting, even though many of them did not like Du Bois's personality and did not agree with him on many issues. The committee worked together for nearly five years, calling their civil-rights activities the Niagara Movement.

But Du Bois's poor relationship with some of the members undermined the organization. This was especially true of William Monroe Trotter, the outspoken editor of the *Guardian* newspaper in Boston, who tried to undermine the group. The organization also ended because the members could not find a way to assist the poor, rural blacks they wanted to help.

In spite of the early disappointment, the organization became the beginning of the National Association for the Advancement of Colored People (NAACP), which Du Bois helped to found in 1910. Some of the NAACP's white founders included reformer Jane Addams and educator John Dewey. The founding members deliberately used the word "colored" in the organization's name because they wanted to make clear they were going to help all dark-skinned people, not just blacks.

As director of research and publicity from 1910 to 1934, Du Bois was the most prominent and visible leader of the NAACP. The NAACP wanted to find ways to stop the anti-black riots in cities throughout the United States. The organization also called upon the U.S. government to put a stop to lynchings. These brutal attacks on black men had become very common after the Civil War and into the first half of the 1900s.

Over the next four decades, the NAACP went through many struggles and conflicts about issues concerning race relations and political power. Du Bois was often at the center of the storm of these internal fights. In

An early supporter of the National Association for the Advancement of Colored People tries to recruit new members to the organization.

the early days of the organization, the NAACP members discussed whether or not to use white support. While Du Bois and the other leaders decided they needed white allies, the organization continued to be run exclusively by black leaders.

In 1919, Du Bois also co-founded the Pan-African Congress, an organization designed to end white supremacy in Africa and increase the rights of black Africans. Du Bois also became the founding editor of the NAACP's influential journal, the *Crisis*, which at its peak had 100,000 subscribers. With the publication of the *Crisis*, he supported many black artists of that time, including writers Langston Hughes and Claude McKay, and opera singer Marian Anderson. Du Bois, Alain Locke, and James Weldon Johnson, who wrote the National Negro Anthem, "Lift Every Voice and Sing," contributed to the "Harlem Renaissance," a term used to describe the numerous artistic and literary works created by black Americans in the Harlem district of New York City during the 1920s.

In 1926, Du Bois had a pioneering role in establishing the Krigwa Players' Little Negro Theater in Harlem. The *Crisis* journal encouraged the community theater to show plays by black authors that depicted black life realistically, and that were written with black audiences in mind. The Krigwa Players became the model for black theater groups throughout the United States in the 1920s and 1930s.

During the Harlem Renaissance, poet Langston Hughes (1902-1967) used jazz-like rhythms and everyday language in his writing to convey the conditions of urban African Americans.

Writer and political activist Claude McKay (1890-1948), another major figure in the 1920s, often discussed racial issues in his poetry.

A third "Renaissance" figure, James Weldon Johnson (1871-1938), a long-time supporter of the NAACP, is perhaps best remembered for his 1912 novel, Autobiography of an Ex-Coloured Man.

Within the NAACP, Du Bois made some enemies, and the organization dismissed him twice. His second dismissal came in 1947 after he had written a memorandum in October 1946 to Walter White, the secretary of the NAACP. In this letter, Du Bois sharply criticized the organization. Du Bois told White that the NAACP must give attention to education, health, politics, and issues affecting black people outside of the United States. Du Bois also criticized the organization's leadership by writing the following:

> We have built in the NAACP a magnificent organization of several hundred thousand persons, but it is not yet a democratic organization, and in our hearts many of us do not believe it can be. We believe in a concentration of power and authority in the hands of a small tight group which issues directives to the mass of members who are expected to be glad to obey. . . . The NAACP should set out to democratize the organization; to hand down and distribute authority to regions and branches and not to concentrate authority in one office or officer; and then to assure progress by searching out intelligent, unselfish, resourceful local leaders of high character and honesty, instead of being content with the prominent and rich who are too often willing to let well enough alone.

Du Bois also said that the NAACP was not doing enough to teach young black people how to read and write. He pointed out that only one-third of the 1946

Walter White (1893-1955) served as secretary for the NAACP from 1931 until his death. His books include a 1948 autobiography entitled A Man Called White.

black army recruits between the ages of 18 and 25 had basic reading and writing skills— a statistic Du Bois found appalling. He also told the leaders of the NAACP that as long as blacks were discriminated against by any government, people of African descent all over the world would never escape the chains of bondage, no matter how free they thought they were.

In addition to his work with the NAACP, Du Bois helped to lead the Peace Information Center, an anti-atomic bomb proliferation group. In the 1950s, his

*During his career,
W.E.B. Du Bois
wrote six
pioneering books
about history,
politics, and race
relations. Two of
the books,* Black
Reconstruction
and The World
and Africa,
*are now considered
classics.*

leadership of this organization made him the target of
staunch anti-communists during the "Cold War" that
began in 1945 following the end of World War II. The
great fear of communism that many people had at that
time made a massive arms build-up seem necessary—and
Du Bois's peace work suspect. Arrested for being an
unregistered foreign agent, a spy, he was tried, but the
jury found him not guilty.

Becoming discouraged with life in the United States,
Du Bois decided to go to the African nation of Ghana in
1961 to help its president, Kwame Nkrumah, edit the
Encyclopaedia Africana. Du Bois remained in Ghana until

his death at age 95. Leaders throughout the world mourned for W.E.B. Du Bois after he died on August 27, 1963—one day before Martin Luther King Jr. would lead the historic March on Washington.

In 1951, Kwame Nkrumah (1909-1972) became the leader of Ghana. The British colony became an independent nation in 1957, and Nkrumah served as president from 1960 to 1966.

After winning several Supreme Court cases as an attorney, Thurgood Marshall (1908-1993) became the first African American appointed to the nation's highest court.

2

Thurgood Marshall
A Champion in the Courtroom

*W*hen Thurgood Marshall was in high school, he was something of a class clown, often telling jokes in class. To punish him for disturbing the class, one of his teachers asked him to memorize sections of the U.S. Constitution, the document that outlines the nation's laws. "I made my way through *every* part of it," he later recalled. Those studies paid off, as Thurgood Marshall later became the first African-American justice of the U.S. Supreme Court. When he died on January 24, 1993, the nation lost one of its most illustrious legal scholars. Through his hard work as an attorney, he forged the ground for advancements in racial equality throughout the United States.

Thurgood was born on July 2, 1908, in Baltimore, Maryland. Thurgood's mother, Norma Marshall, worked as an elementary school teacher and encouraged her son to be tactful, hardworking, and inquisitive. His father, William Marshall, was an intelligent man, but he had little education and worked as a waiter. Thurgood learned self-respect and dignity from his father.

As an adult, Thurgood Marshall would recall his father telling him, "Anyone calls you nigger, you not only got my permission to fight him—you got my orders to fight him." But young Thurgood never did much fighting with his fists. Instead, he told jokes. By using tact, he got more information from a casual conversation than most lawyers could obtain from a legal brief (a written summary of a legal case).

After graduating from high school in 1925, Marshall moved to Philadelphia to attend all-black Lincoln University, where he became a star debater. Just before the start of his senior year, he married Vivian Burey, a student at the University of Pennsylvania. In the spring of 1930, Marshall earned a humanities degree and graduated from college with honors.

Later that year, the Marshalls relocated to Washington, D.C., where Thurgood attended law school at Howard University, the nation's largest predominantly black university. To help pay for his tuition, his mother pawned her wedding and engagement rings. Marshall thanked her by studying hard and being named the top student in his class during his first year in law school.

Charles Hamilton Houston, vice-dean of Howard's law school and one of Marshall's professors, had built a reputation as a brilliant lawyer and a pioneer civil rights activist. Houston had reorganized the university's law school to be an effective training ground for African Americans who wanted to use the law to bring about social change. Houston was tough on his students. Although Marshall did not initially understand why his professor always seemed so disagreeable, he later spoke favorably of Houston:

> He used to tell us that doctors could bury their mistakes, but lawyers couldn't. And he'd drive home to us that we would be competing not only with white lawyers but really well-trained white lawyers, so there just wasn't any point in crying in our beer about being Negroes. And I'll tell you, the going was rough. There must have been 30 of us in that class when we started, and no more than 8 or 10 of us finished up. We used to call him "Iron Shoes" and "Pants" and a few other names that don't bear repeating. But he was a sweet man once you saw what he was up to. He was absolutely fair, and the door to his office was always open. He made it clear to all of us that when we were done, we were expected to go out and do something with our lives.

Houston thought that the only worthy role for a lawyer was that of social engineer—someone who understood the U.S. Constitution and knew how to use it to improve the living conditions of underprivileged citizens. That was the kind of lawyer he wanted Howard University to produce, and that was precisely the kind of lawyer that Marshall wanted to become.

In 1933, Thurgood Marshall became valedictorian of Howard University's School of Law graduating class. Eager to begin practicing law, he turned down a full scholarship to pursue post-graduate studies at Harvard University. After passing the Maryland state bar examination, he opened a law office in Baltimore, Maryland. Because few black people had enough money to pay for legal services, Marshall did only *pro bono* work during his first year as an attorney. That is, he did not require any of his clients to pay for his services. After he won many of his early cases to help less fortunate people, Marshall's colleagues began calling him "the little man's lawyer."

The Baltimore chapter of the National Association for the Advancement of Colored People (NAACP) heard about Marshall's success and asked him to work for the organization. This opportunity exhilarated Marshall. Professor Houston had already been working for the NAACP, often traveling through southern states to film teachers, students, classrooms, and school buses. Houston called his documentary *Examples of Educational Discrimination Among Rural Negroes in South Carolina*, and

As a lawyer for the NAACP, Thurgood Marshall (pictured here in front of the U.S. Supreme Court building) believed that racist practices were against the law according to the U.S. Constitution.

he used this film when he spoke at college campuses and NAACP events.

In 1935, Houston had become the first African American to win a case before the U.S. Supreme Court for the NAACP. In *Hollins v. State of Oklahoma*, Houston convinced the nation's highest court to overturn the conviction of a black man on the grounds that African Americans had been illegally excluded from the jury. As special counsel for the NAACP, Houston also shed light on the unconstitutionality of *Plessy v. Ferguson*, the Supreme Court ruling of 1896 that had legalized the "separate but equal" segregation system known informally as "Jim Crow" (from a 19th-century minstrel song).

By the 1930s, "Jim Crow" had become a household phrase in the United States. City, county, and state laws prohibited black people from drinking from the same water fountains, eating at the same restaurants, attending the same schools, or using the same public restrooms as whites. Furthermore, when blacks passed whites on the street, they were expected to nod their heads or tip their hats. But whites did not have to remove their hats even when they entered a black person's home. Blacks had to address whites as "Sir" or "Ma'am." Yet whites could call blacks by their first names—no matter how old they were.

In 1935, Marshall heard about a young man named Donald Gaines Murray who had been denied admission to the University of Maryland's all-white law school because he was black. Houston and Marshall teamed up to fight "Jim Crow," and Houston argued the case in Baltimore's city court. If the state of Maryland had no black law schools, he said, then Maryland's black residents should be allowed to attend an all-white law school. Marshall and Houston won the Murray case, and it became an important victory for the NAACP's legal campaign. Together, the two men had forced a white graduate school to accept a black student.

Marshall and Houston periodically traveled throughout the South during the mid-1930s, gathering evidence and meeting with regional NAACP officers to search for other cases they could use to challenge "Jim Crow" laws. To further demonstrate that separate facilities for blacks and whites were unequal, Houston argued and won *Gaines v. Missouri* in 1938. The Supreme Court ruling in this case forced the University of Missouri to change its policy of providing a law school for white students, but not for blacks. The case set a precedent for future "separate but equal" cases. The men also won decisions in *Hurd v. Hodge* and *Shelley v. Kraemer*, which made racially segregated housing illegal.

After five years of working as the NAACP's chief legal counsel, Houston left in 1938 to go back into private practice. By now one of the nation's most prominent black attorneys, Marshall took over a position at the association's national headquarters in New York City. He helped form the NAACP Legal Defense and Education

Fund, which provided free legal counsel to needy blacks who had suffered racial injustice.

In 1940, Marshall prepared to present his first case before the Supreme Court. In *Chambers v. Florida*, Marshall argued that the convictions of three black men accused of murdering white men were unjust because the police had forced the men to confess after five days of nonstop questioning. He successfully argued that this technique was a violation of the "due process" clause in the U.S. Constitution that was designed to protect an individual's rights during legal proceedings.

Marshall then challenged an illegal device designed to keep blacks from voting. In southern states, the candidates who won during the primaries almost always won in the elections. Since blacks were not allowed to belong to political parties, they could not vote in the primary elections, which gave them minimal influence in the outcome of elections. Marshall went before the U.S. Supreme Court to argue that this practice was unconstitutional. Once again, he won a case before the Court.

Marshall's most important victory came next. In 1954, Marshall became the NAACP's lead attorney in the school desegregation case of *Brown v. Board of Education of Topeka*, which he would argue before the U.S. Supreme Court. During the early 1950s, the NAACP had asked several black families in the South to try enrolling their students in all-white public schools. When not one of the black students was admitted, the NAACP brought the

*Students attend an all-black school during the early
1900s. Five decades would pass before public schools
would be desegregated.*

case to court. The organization spent $100,000 preparing
the lawsuit, which was consolidated with similar segregation cases by the time the Supreme Court made its ruling.

Although the Supreme Court justices handed down
their decision in the *Brown* case four years after Houston's
death, Marshall fully credited his old teacher and team-
mate with engineering the legal strategy that had struck
down racial segregation in public schools. Marshall had
argued that segregation was inherently unconstitutional

After Linda Brown and several other black students were not allowed to enroll in segregated public schools, the NAACP filed a lawsuit on behalf of their families. Linda's father, Oliver Brown, was one of the parents who participated in the landmark Brown v. Board of Education of Topeka *desegregation case.*

because it disgraced an entire race. He also argued that segregation laws denied blacks "equal protection of laws" as guaranteed by the Fourteenth Amendment. The U.S. Supreme Court agreed with him.

In its decision, the Supreme Court said, "We conclude unanimously, that in the field of education the doctrine of 'separate but equal' has no place. Separate educational facilities are inherently unequal." This judgment may have been the most important legal decision in the civil rights movement. It not only reversed the 1896 *Plessy v. Ferguson* case that had made "separate but equal" legal, but it would also serve as a legal precedent for future cases that would prohibit segregation in other areas.

The Court's decision was headline news. That week's edition of *Time* magazine reported, "In its 164 years, the Court had erected many a landmark of U.S. history . . . none of them except the *Dred Scott* case (reversed by the Civil War) was more important than the school segregation issue. None of them directly and intimately affected so many American families."

Black people across the United States rejoiced when the Court delivered its ruling on Monday, May 17, 1954. Marshall, the lawyer who had argued and won the case, remained subdued while his friends and colleagues

In 1857, the Supreme Court declared that even though slave Dred Scott had been brought to the North, where slavery was then prohibited, he still belonged to his white master.

celebrated. Perhaps he knew that this case was only the beginning of what was yet to come.

The *Brown* decision caused a backlash. White segregationists called that day "Black Monday" to show their disapproval. President Dwight Eisenhower distanced himself from the Court's decision, saying that it did not matter whether or not he endorsed the ruling. But Eisenhower later told one of his White House aides that he was convinced the Court decision pushed race relations in the South back by at least 15 years. As a result of the ruling, angry whites assaulted and murdered black citizens in increasing numbers.

For Marshall, the joy of the Court's ruling was further shattered when he learned that his wife, Vivian, was dying of lung cancer. After her death in 1955, Marshall married another woman, Cecilia Suyat, and the couple had two sons.

Marshall continued his civil rights battles in the courtroom throughout the 1950s. He fought segregation in the schools, helped Martin Luther King Jr. and other civil rights activists attract more support, and opposed southern efforts to ban the NAACP. Still, some people criticized him, saying he should take a more active role in King's freedom crusades.

By 1961, Marshall had argued 32 cases before the U.S. Supreme Court and had won 29 of them. In September of that year, President John F. Kennedy appointed him to the Second Circuit Court of Appeals,

In 1957, President Dwight Eisenhower ordered federal troops to escort nine black students into the newly desegregated Central High School in Little Rock because Arkansas's governor had ordered the state troops to stop the students from entering.

the most prestigious court in New York State. During his four years as a judge on that court, Marshall ruled on approximately 1,600 cases, and the U.S. Supreme Court never overturned any of his opinions. This incredible record led to his appointment as the first African-American U.S. solicitor general, the chief assistant to the U.S. attorney general. As the nation's top-ranking courtroom advocate, Marshall won 14 of his 19 cases, most of which involved civil rights or privacy issues.

Marshall made history again in 1967, when President Lyndon B. Johnson nominated him to the U.S. Supreme Court. When the U.S. Senate approved his nomination that August, Marshall became the first African American to sit on the high court. In that post, he defended individual human rights, as well as educational and racial equality for all people. Because he believed that capital punishment (the death penalty) was inherently unfair and tainted with racism, Marshall never voted to put a criminal to death.

In 1991, failing health caused Marshall to step down from the U.S. Supreme Court. In January 1993, he died of heart failure at Bethesda Naval Medical Center in

Only white men had served on the Supreme Court before 1967, when President Johnson nominated Thurgood Marshall. The 1967 Court included (from left to right) John M. Harlan, Abe Fortas, Hugo Black, Potter Stewart, Earl Warren (chief justice), Byron White, William O. Douglas, Thurgood Marshall, and William J. Brennan.

The Supreme Court became more diverse during Thurgood Marshall's 24 years as a justice. Serving on the Court in 1991 were (from left to right) Harry Blackmun, Anthony Kennedy, Byron White, Sandra Day O'Connor, William Rehnquist (chief justice), Antonin Scalia, Thurgood Marshall, David Souter, and John Paul Stevens.

Maryland at the age of 84. While delivering his eulogy at Marshall's funeral service, Chief Justice William Rehnquist said the following about the late Justice Marshall:

> As a result of his career as a lawyer and as a judge, Thurgood Marshall left an indelible mark, not just upon the law, but upon his country. Inscribed above the front entrance to the Supreme Court building are the words "equal justice under law." Surely no one individual did more to make these words a reality than Thurgood Marshall.

Civil rights leader James Farmer established CORE in 1942, an organization that helped to end many racist practices in the United States.

3

James Farmer
Leader of the Freedom Rides

*A*lmost every Sunday while James Farmer was growing up, his family would pack a picnic lunch and head out for a long drive in the hilly countryside outside Austin, Texas. During one of these drives, his father accidentally hit a pig that wandered into the road. Although the pig squealed loudly, his father did not stop the car. "Out in these rural parts, Negroes are killed for less," his father said.

When the family found a spot to have their picnic, James's mother spread a tablecloth on a grassy place near the road, then brought out the fried chicken, hard-boiled eggs, potato salad, and lemonade. As James bit into a chicken drumstick, two white men approached the area in a black pickup truck. One of them held a shotgun and accused James's father of killing his pig. He demanded that James's father pay him $45 for the pig. Mr. Farmer had no cash with him, but he offered to give the man his $57 paycheck. When he handed his accuser the check, the white man let it fall to the ground.

"Pick it up, nigger," he said.

James watched silently. "Don't do it, Daddy," he said to himself. "Don't pick it up. He dropped it. Let him pick it up." But Mr. Farmer bent over and picked up the check, then he handed it to the white man. At that time, James decided he would never give in to that kind of intimidation.

James Leonard Farmer Jr. was born on January 12, 1920, in Marshall, Texas. His father, one of the first African Americans to earn a doctoral degree in that state, was a minister of a Methodist church in the town of Marshall. James Leonard Farmer Sr., whom everyone called J. Leonard, could read Latin, Greek, French, German, Hebrew, and Aramaic.

Soon after James Jr. was born, his family moved from Marshall, Texas, to Holly Springs, Mississippi, where J. Leonard taught at Rust College, a school for blacks. Not long afterward, the family moved to Austin, where J. Leonard became professor of religion and philosophy at Samuel Houston College (now Houston-Tillotson College).

James Jr. entered the first grade shortly before he turned five. A bright child, James already knew how to read and write before he started school. Within a few weeks, he was promoted to the second grade. He won several speech contests in high school, and his high marks earned him a four-year college scholarship. James Farmer graduated from high school at the young age of 14 and entered Wiley College in Marshall in 1934.

While James Farmer was growing up during the early 1900s, segregated drinking fountains, buses, restrooms, and other public facilities were common in the South.

African Americans knew they could be arrested for drinking out of a fountain marked "white" or for using other facilities that weren't intended for "colored" people.

In college, Farmer decided to find a way to fight the segregation that he had witnessed as a child. "My ambition was to wage war on racism," he later said. But at that time, he did not know precisely how to fight that battle. After graduating from Wiley College in 1938, Farmer moved to Washington, D.C., where he attended Howard University and studied to become a minister. At Howard, Farmer learned about Mohandas Gandhi, a lawyer and spiritual leader from India who was using nonviolent resistance to free his people from British rule.

Farmer realized Gandhi's peaceful methods might also work to end segregation in the South. Other students at Howard shared his belief. Soon these students and Farmer became active in an organization called the Fellowship of Reconciliation (FOR), which was dedicated to nonviolent social change.

Around this time, Farmer began to speak his mind, including his belief that all wars were immoral. In June 1941, President Franklin D. Roosevelt invited Farmer and a group of other students to the White House. During the visit, Farmer boldly spoke to the president about his opposition to war. When the United States entered World War II that December, Farmer publicly spoke out against the nation's involvement in the conflict.

Farmer also began to study the relationship between race and religion. This led him to believe that although churches were supposed to be holy, they often had racist practices, such as presenting religion from a

Eurocentric viewpoint and excluding blacks from involvement in some church activities. Because of this, Farmer decided not to become a minister. Instead, when he graduated from Howard's divinity school in 1941, James decided to work at the Chicago branch of FOR. He earned $15 a week and traveled across the United States making antiwar speeches.

Before moving to Chicago, Farmer had thought that racism existed only in the South, but he soon learned that most blacks in northern cities also lived in separate neighborhoods from whites. Many northern whites did not want blacks to eat in certain restaurants or to shop at certain stores.

Farmer decided to take action against racial segregation and discrimination wherever he found it. He spoke to college students throughout the midwestern and southern regions of the United States. In 1942, he came up with a desegregation plan called "Brotherhood Mobilization," which was based on Gandhi's principles of nonviolence and love.

In April 1942, forty people met and started the Committee of Racial Equality (CORE). Of the six key people responsible for founding CORE, four were white and two were black. They were all Christian activists who believed in using nonviolent methods to support social change. The two black founders were George Houser and Joe Guinn. As a third-year theological student, Houser had been sentenced to prison for refusing to register for the draft. After spending a year in prison, he began working as a part-time field officer for FOR. Joe Guinn, a student at the University of Chicago, was also later imprisoned for not fighting in the war. Guinn was head of the local NAACP Youth Council.

The 40 people who met to form CORE selected Farmer as their first national director. FOR members all over the United States began forming local CORE chapters. In June 1943, CORE held its first national meeting. Farmer called for "interracial, nonviolent direct action" against racial segregation. CORE became one the four organizations that were the backbone of the civil rights movement of the 1960s. The other three organizations were the National Association for the Advancement of Colored People (NAACP), the Southern Christian Leadership Conference (SCLC), and the Student Nonviolent Coordinating Committee (SNCC).

Farmer began leading successful protests, and he gained national attention for criticizing restaurants in Chicago that refused to serve black people. As more people joined CORE, the group changed its name to the Congress of Racial Equality in 1944. By this time, some CORE members had started arguing with each other because they did not like Farmer's ideas for massive protests and some of his opinions about which direction the organization should take. To put an end to these arguments, Farmer resigned as CORE's national director and stayed away from the organization for the next 17 years.

After leaving CORE, Farmer continued fighting racial segregation and hatred. For several years, he worked to organize labor unions, but he finally got back into the fight for civil rights in 1959. At that time, he became program director for the NAACP, the nation's oldest and largest civil rights organization. When Farmer first accepted this position, he was happy to be back in the civil rights movement. But he felt out of place in the NAACP, an organization that waged most of its battles in the nation's courtrooms. Its lawyers, including George E.C. Hayes, James Nabrit Jr., and Thurgood Marshall, had won many victories against racism. Marshall's victory in the 1954 landmark *Brown v. Board of Education of Topeka* Supreme Court case outlawed racial segregation in public schools.

In early 1961, CORE began looking for a new national director. The organization tried to hire Martin Luther King Jr., who had led thousands of people in Montgomery, Alabama, in a nonviolent boycott of the city's segregated bus system. Because he felt that continuing to lead nonviolent protests would be more effective than working for CORE, King respectfully declined the position.

Farmer, on the other hand, jumped at the opportunity to head CORE again. During his 17-year absence, the organization had continued fighting segregation, but it had not always been very effective. The group did not have much money, and its members had not been able to generate the kind of attention that King and his followers had been enjoying. Farmer knew he could do a good job and breathe new life into CORE. On February 1, 1961, he resumed his old position. That same year, a Supreme Court decision made it illegal to designate separate "white" waiting rooms and "colored" waiting rooms in bus and train stations. Unfortunately, many places in the South ignored this law and continued to offer only segregated facilities.

To promote this new ruling, Farmer came up with the idea of "freedom riders." He planned to have groups of peaceful protesters ride throughout the South. These protesters would stop at segregated restaurants, bus stations, and restrooms, and they would ignore the racist signs. The freedom riders gave CORE the national attention it sought.

On May 4, 1961, 13 freedom riders split into two groups and started traveling through the South. At first, they experienced no trouble and found no racist signs in some of the depots they visited. But as they traveled deeper into the South, the situation changed.

Meanwhile, in Anniston, Alabama, a white mob carrying clubs and iron bars attacked a Greyhound bus carrying the freedom riders. The mob smashed the bus windows and slashed the tires. The driver was able to take the bus out of town, but the mob followed the bus

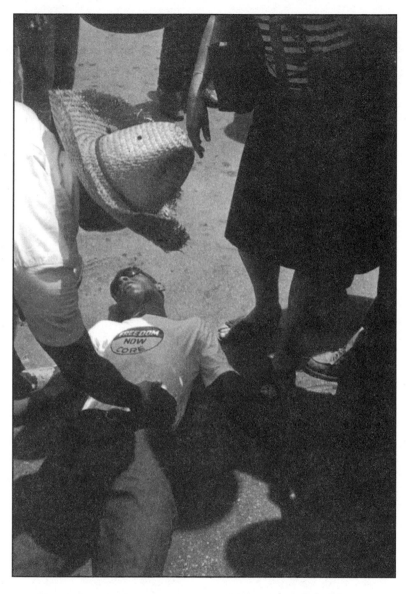

During a civil rights demonstration in 1963, this CORE member was knocked to the ground by someone opposed to the movement. Many other civil rights activists were injured during the turbulent 1960s.

and firebombed it. When the second group of freedom riders reached Birmingham, Alabama, a group of 40 white people was waiting for them. The Birmingham police let the white mob beat the riders with lead pipes, baseball bats, and tire chains for 15 minutes.

Because his father, J. Leonard, had died on May 13, 1961, Farmer had left the freedom riders the day before these two attacks. But when he heard about the attacks, he quickly canceled the rest of the trip for the two groups out of fear for their lives. Soon afterward, Farmer met with Martin Luther King Jr. in Montgomery and helped him calm more than 1,000 angry black people, who were tired of violence against them and were ready to fight back. The two peacemakers quieted the storm and together decided to get back aboard the buses. On May 24, the freedom riders were back on the move. This time, they had the help of the National Guard.

In Jackson, Mississippi, Farmer was the first one off the bus and led the group into the bus station. When the freedom riders went inside the depot, the police chief said he would arrest them if they didn't leave. Despite this threat, the freedom riders ignored the racist signs in the depot and stayed. Because Farmer and his freedom riders had broken a segregation law, the police chief arrested them. U.S. attorney general Robert Kennedy arranged for them to pay a small fine rather than remain in jail. But Farmer and the other protesters stayed in jail for six weeks, refusing to pay the fine. They had little to

While serving as U.S. attorney general from 1961 to 1964, Robert Kennedy (1925-1968) supported many social reforms and became a strong advocate of the civil rights movement.

eat and endured the filthy jail to make their point that segregation was wrong and they were right.

The city of Jackson, Mississippi, released Farmer and the other activists on July 7. Farmer returned as a hero to CORE's national office in New York City. By the end of the summer of 1961, more than 1,000 people had participated in the freedom rides. This nonviolent protest helped CORE become one of the major civil rights organizations in the United States. Under Farmer's direction, CORE went on to fight discrimination in labor unions and to sponsor programs for better housing and education in areas where black people lived.

Farmer resigned from CORE in 1966, hoping to turn his attention to the political arena. He ran unsuccessfully for Congress in 1968. The following year, President Richard Nixon appointed him assistant secretary of the Department of Health, Education, and Welfare. Because this job involved government bureaucracy, which Farmer had opposed for so many years, he did not enjoy the position and resigned in 1970.

Farmer continued his fight against racism throughout the 1970s. He worked in Washington, D.C., until 1979, when a rare eye disease caused his vision to deteriorate slowly. In 1985, still battling blindness, Farmer became a history professor at Mary Washington College in Fredericksburg, Virginia, where he continues to teach students to fight against racism.

In the 1960s, James Farmer addresses a crowd about the need for the federal government to become more involved in the civil rights movement.

Through her thoughtfulness and persistence, Ella Baker (1903-1986) helped to motivate many young adults to join the civil rights movement.

4

Ella Baker
The "Othermother" of Civil Rights

*E*ven when Ella Baker was a young girl growing up in the South, she liked telling others what to do. One time, when she was about 11 years old, she chased a widowed farmer's young children through the fields and tackled them just so she could give them a bath and provide them with clean clothes. As an adult, Baker would sometimes be called the "othermother" because of the guidance she provided for her younger colleagues in the civil rights movement.

Ella Baker was born on December 13, 1903, to Georgianna and Blake Baker in Norfolk, Virginia. She had an older brother named Curtis and a younger sister named Margaret. While growing up, Ella was both courageous and tough. Although the world was filled with racial hatred, she did not feel inferior to white people. At age six, she slapped a white boy for calling her a "nigger."

When Ella was eight, she moved to Littleton, North Carolina, with her mother and siblings. Her mother worked as a school teacher in the town. Blake Baker remained in Virginia, however, to keep his job as a waiter on a ferryboat. He wrote to his family often, but he was able to see his wife and children only three or four times each year.

Everyone in Littleton relied upon each other for survival, sharing farm equipment, food, and money. "If there were emergencies, the farmer next to you would share something to meet that emergency," Ella would later say. It was here that she first learned to care for other people. The Baker family shared fruits and vegetables from their large garden with their neighbors. Ella's mother took care of sick people in their area and raised two homeless boys from the community.

Ella attended a small public school for black children in Littleton. Her mother encouraged all three of her children to do well in school because she believed that education was the best way to prepare for a productive life. At that time, many black children were unable to go to school because they had to work full time to help their families. Those who did attend school often had to drop out after the third grade in order to take care of their younger siblings or to assist with the farm work.

Georgianna sent Ella to Raleigh, North Carolina, where she attended high school and then enrolled at Shaw University. To help earn money for college, Ella waited tables and worked as an assistant in a chemistry laboratory on campus. A school policy prohibited young men and women from walking across the campus together. Ella wrote a letter to the school officials protesting this policy, and she persuaded them to get rid of the rule.

When Baker had entered Shaw, she thought she would become a medical missionary or a social worker. But she changed her mind when she learned that the advanced training required for these professions would be very expensive. When she graduated from Shaw in 1927, Baker moved to the Harlem district of New York City to find a job.

In New York City, Baker again waited tables, and later worked in a factory. She also wrote articles for black-owned newspapers in Harlem. Newspapers run by whites wrote very few stories about African Americans, and the stories they did publish were usually only about black people committing crimes. In her articles, Baker tried to present a more diverse and realistic picture of the lives of black people in New York City and the rest of the United States.

At the time, the Harlem Renaissance was at its peak, as many black people in that area were engaging in artistic endeavors and discussing the important issues of the time. Baker took part in these lively discussions and developed ideas about how she could help her people make important changes in the world.

When the Great Depression hit the United States in 1929, millions of Americans of all races lost their jobs and went hungry. In the midst of those troubled times, Baker found her calling. In 1932, she helped start a food cooperative project in her community. While helping to buy food wholesale, she became an expert at consumer affairs. A few years later, Baker landed a job at the Works Progress Administration (WPA) to help others hurt by the Depression. (The WPA, one of the first social-aid programs in the United States, had been established by President Franklin D. Roosevelt in 1933.)

Baker's role as a social activist began in 1938 when she joined the National Association for the Advancement of Colored People (NAACP) as an assistant field secretary. The organization sent her to other NAACP branches throughout the South. She was on the road about half the time, trying to persuade people to join in the battle for civil rights. NAACP members had usually been black professionals, doctors, business owners, teachers, and lawyers, but now the organization was working to get ordinary people involved in the NAACP. She wanted janitors, street cleaners, construction workers, gardeners, and housekeepers to join the organization. She felt they were the people who needed the NAACP the most.

In 1942, Baker became the NAACP's director of branches. In this position, she managed the activities of the local chapters of the organization in cities across the country. She helped them to organize membership drives and raise money. She showed them how to solve local problems, such as getting new traffic lights installed.

Baker resigned from her position with the NAACP in 1946 because she needed to be at home to take care of her eight-year-old niece, Jackie. Jackie had been born in Littleton, but her parents asked Baker—with her college education and world experience—to raise their daughter in New York. (It was a common practice during this period for African-American children to be raised by relatives other than their parents.) Baker now took time out to help Jackie become accustomed to New York. She bought her niece new clothes and enrolled her in school.

But Baker missed being involved in the community. Within one year after leaving the NAACP, she opened the first branch of the American Cancer Society in Harlem. This organization provided information about the causes of cancer and how to recognize the early signs of the disease. Baker also became involved in community organizations that assisted Harlem's poor residents.

Baker later rejoined the NAACP, and became president of the organization's New York City branch in 1954. Her involvement with the NAACP led her back to the South the next year, as thousands of black people had begun boycotting the buses in Montgomery, Alabama.

In 1956, Martin Luther King Jr. and his followers successfully concluded the one-year bus boycott in Montgomery, which had attracted national attention. At that time, Baker insisted that the spirit and momentum of the civil rights movement not be allowed to die just because the white officials in Montgomery had finally let blacks sit wherever they pleased in buses, instead of only being allowed to sit at the back of the bus.

Baker said that the movement needed a central organization to mobilize black people and keep the boycott momentum going. She advised leaders of the bus strike to begin using their skills for other civil rights projects.

King told Baker that after a major demonstration like the year-long bus boycott, people needed to have time to catch their breath. But Baker disagreed. She asked King to meet with her and several members of an organization called "In Friendship." Baker and others, including Bayard Rustin and Stanley Levison, convinced King that they could continue the success of the boycott.

On January 11, 1957, King called a meeting of more than 60 black ministers and community leaders in the South, which led to the formation of the Southern Christian Leadership Conference (SCLC). Baker

Ella Baker (far right) attends a civil rights meeting during the mid-1900s.

accepted the position of the SCLC's first acting director while the board of directors looked for someone else to become the administrator. One of the first major missions the SCLC undertook was encouraging more black people to register to vote.

Baker encouraged the SCLC to sponsor a conference to teach students how to be activists. This conference led to the formation of the Student Nonviolent Coordinating Committee (SNCC, usually pronounced "snick").

Historians sometimes refer to Baker as the mother of the civil rights movement since she served as a political "midwife" at the births of both the Southern Christian Leadership Conference and the Student Nonviolent Coordinating Committee, as well as other civil rights organizations.

Baker was one of the people who headed the mission called the "Crusade for Citizenship." The group planned to hold rallies in 22 southern cities on February 12, 1958. When the group still had no one to coordinate the rallies by the end of January, Baker decided to do the job. Within weeks, she had contacted ministers in all 22 cities, informing them about the rallies and suggesting that they tell their congregation members about this plan for voter registration. She also sent the churches information packages about civil rights activities and voter registration laws.

Voter registration drives became an important way to advance the civil rights movement in the late 1950s and 1960s.

The drives were not very successful in getting large numbers of people out to vote. Baker criticized the leaders for not doing a good enough job of promoting the movement and for not allowing young people to become more involved. Unfortunately, many of the older and more experienced civil rights workers had doubted the ability of the young to work independently from their own groups.

Baker told the young adults who were active in SNCC not to become intimidated by older members. She taught the younger members that everyone had something important to say, regardless of age. Following Baker's beliefs, SNCC came up with its first slogan: "We are all leaders," and Baker earned her nickname as the "othermother."

No one could pull rank on Baker, not even Martin Luther King Jr. When the students began physically fighting over the issue of whether to hold sit-ins against segregated facilities or to concentrate on voter registration, Baker stopped the fight by explaining to them how they could do both. (The first sit-in was held in Greensboro, North Carolina, where college students protested segregated lunch counters by peacefully sitting in seats reserved for whites.)

Some SNCC members became involved in the freedom rides that James Farmer organized in the 1960s, when teams of blacks and whites traveled together throughout the South on buses, visiting bus stations, restaurants, and other public places to challenge segregation laws. Members of SNCC learned that the voter registration drives could be just as dangerous as freedom riding and could draw as much attention as the sit-ins and freedom rides had done. SNCC members kept a log of how many times its members faced life-threatening situations in Mississippi; from the end of 1961 to the beginning of 1964, they counted 150 violent incidents.

In 1964, more than 800 white students had volunteered to work on Freedom Summer. A special school in Oxford, Ohio, taught these volunteers nonviolent resistance and procedures for voter registration. After a week of training, 300 students set out on June 20, 1964. The next day, three of the civil rights workers—Andrew Goodman, James Chaney, and Michael Schwerner—disappeared while working on a voter registration project. Chaney was black, and Goodman and Schwerner were white.

Approximately 400 military officers and FBI agents searched the South for the three volunteers. The FBI eventually found their bodies buried on a farm just outside the town of Philadelphia, Mississippi. All three had been shot to death. Twenty-one men, including a county sheriff and a deputy sheriff, were arrested in connection with the murders. An all-white jury in Mississippi found the 21 men not guilty of the crimes. A federal court later tried the case and sent 7 of the men to prison.

(Left to right) Michael Schwerner, James Chaney, and Andrew Goodman—three casualties of the civil rights movement

Soon after the three students disappeared, President Lyndon Johnson signed into law the Civil Rights Act of 1964, which made it illegal to deny jobs to blacks or to prevent them from entering public places.

Ella Baker was also a guiding force behind the formation of the Mississippi Freedom Democratic Party (MFDP), which later challenged President Johnson to move even faster in the drive for racial equality. Baker's leadership in that movement brought about changes in the political process, including the way party delegates were selected. At this time, Baker returned to New York and resumed her work in the black community, seeking better housing and job opportunities for black people who lived in Harlem. In the early 1970s, she held rallies to raise money for the black people living in the southern African nation of Rhodesia. Eventually, the blacks of

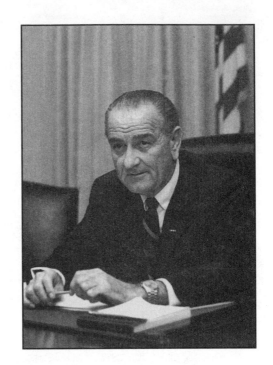

As part of his Great Society plan for the United States, Democratic president Lyndon Johnson (1908–1973) supported educational reforms, economic programs, and civil rights legislation. Johnson held office from 1963 to 1969.

Rhodesia (now called Zimbabwe) overthrew their white-run government.

Baker also worked in the struggle for freedom in South Africa and with the leading black South African freedom organization, the African National Congress (ANC), which had formed in 1912. When members of the ANC visited New York, Baker helped them to raise money for their cause.

In her later years, Ella Baker received the recognition she had always tried to avoid. For her 75th birthday in 1978, the Coalition of 100 Black Women threw a party in New York City in her honor. In 1984, the organization presented her with its Candace Award for outstanding achievement.

Ella Baker died in New York City on December 13, 1986, her 83rd birthday. During her lifetime, she gave thousands of people the courage to join the ranks of the NAACP. She shaped the SCLC with her ability to organize and she helped SNCC to become one of the strongest forces in the civil rights movement.

Baker became a role model for both white and black women. Her name has been placed alongside Nelson Mandela's to form the Baker/Mandela Center for Anti-Racist Education at the University of Michigan. Through her words and her actions, Baker left a mark not only on the United States but also on the world. "I believe the struggle is eternal," she once said. "Somebody else carries on."

Nelson Mandela was convicted of treason in his native South Africa in 1964 for participating in a campaign to end apartheid, South Africa's policy of racial segregation. Mandela was released in 1990 and became the country's first black president in 1994.

Andrew Young faced many struggles during his years as a civil rights activist and public official, but he has always remained optimistic about the future.

5

Andrew Young
An Ambassador for Human Rights

*A*ndrew Jackson Young Jr. had to learn how to fight at an early age. Andrew's father gave him boxing lessons so he could defend himself from neighborhood bullies. He set up a boxing ring in their yard and hired the best boxer in the area to train his son. Soon afterward, young Andrew's father told him, "Don't get mad, get smart." Years later, Young came to realize that boxing was not the best way to protect himself. "I learned that negotiating was better than fighting," he said.

As an adult, Andrew Young would become a powerful negotiator in the nonviolent civil rights movement. He worked side by side with Martin Luther King Jr. in the Southern Christian Leadership Conference (SCLC), promoting sit-ins, marches, and boycotts in northern and southern states. Young drafted legislation in Congress that made it possible for blacks to share the same rights as white Americans. He was also the first African American to serve as U.S. ambassador to the United Nations.

Andrew Jackson Young Jr. was born on March 12, 1932, in New Orleans, Louisiana. He was the oldest of Andrew Young Sr. and Daisy Fuller Young's two sons. His father was a dentist and his mother taught school.

Because of these two professional jobs, the Youngs could give their sons things the other children in the neighborhood did not have. Andrew and his brother, Walter, grew up much better off than many black people of that time. While other black children in the segregated South had to attend "colored only" movie theaters, Andrew's parents took him and his brother on a trip to New York City, where they visited movie theaters, parks, and restaurants that served both whites and blacks. Some of their friends—both black and white—were jealous of Andrew and Walter because they had much nicer clothes and toys than most children.

Andrew was a very intelligent child and entered first grade when he was only four. But school bored him, and he didn't work very hard on his assignments. Andrew's parents worried that he was only doing enough to get by.

Although he was not interested in school, Andrew loved reading. While his classmates were learning about former presidents George Washington and Thomas Jefferson, Andrew began reading about people such as Ralph Bunche, the first African American to earn a Ph.D. in political science from Harvard. Bunche was also the first African American to hold an executive position with the U.S. Department of State, and in 1950 he became the first African American to win the Nobel Peace Prize. He received this international award for his work in getting warring Egypt and Israel to cease hostilities in 1949. Andrew Young considered Bunche a hero, and he would later try to emulate him in many ways.

Growing up in a religious family, Andrew attended Sunday school and was a member of the youth choir. When his grandmother later became blind, Andrew and his brother sat with her and read to her from the Bible. Andrew always had great compassion for other people. As a child, he asked his parents to take him to visit some of the elderly people in his community because he realized they were old and lonely and would appreciate having some company.

In 1947, when he was 15, Andrew graduated from Gilbert Academy, a private high school in New Orleans. Feeling Andrew was too young to go away to college, his parents initially made him attend college close to home at the all-black Dillard University in New Orleans. After his freshman year, Andrew Young transferred to Howard University, a prestigious black college in Washington, D.C., that had already prepared many other notable African Americans for work in civil rights.

Young was smaller and younger than most of his peers at Howard University, but he made the swimming and track teams his senior year. In later life, he recalled that he was different from many students, who put partying first and school second. Young later said he put athletics first, partying second, and school third. Because of his poor study habits, Young was only a mediocre student. His parents feared that his biology grades were not high enough to get him into a good dental school, like the one Andrew Sr. had attended.

When he was 19, Young went through a troubling time. Dissatisfied with other people's high expectations of him, he decided to change his goals in life. But he did not have another goal to replace dentistry. Although he had once loved going to fraternity parties, he now began to view them as trivial. He even began to think his steady girlfriend was too materialistic.

After graduating from Howard in 1951, Young returned home to New Orleans with an uncertain future. He was a college graduate, but he did not know very much—except how to have fun. On the way home from school, Young met a young man who planned to go to the African nation of Angola to help the black people of that

Portuguese colony. This man's dedication changed Young's outlook on life, and he spent his first summer after college working for the United Christian Youth Movement. The organization sent him to Indiana for training, and then on to Rhode Island and Connecticut to work as an activist. This was the beginning of the work that would make Andrew Young famous. That summer, Young learned how important it was to help others. He discovered that he loved working with teenagers of all backgrounds and races. By the time he finished his volunteer assignment in Connecticut, he decided that he wanted to become a minister.

Young enrolled at Hartford Theological Seminary in Hartford, Connecticut, to prepare for the ministry. While there, he began reading about Mohandas Gandhi, the famous religious leader who led the people of India in their struggle for independence from Great Britain during the late 1940s. Gandhi's beliefs also had a profound effect on other great civil rights leaders such as Martin Luther King Jr. and James Farmer, who had adopted Gandhi's teaching of "passive resistance." Gandhi believed that activists should only use nonviolent tactics—such as peaceful demonstrations and boycotts—to persuade officials to reform unfair laws or policies.

For all of his life, Young had thought that physically fighting back was the right way to defeat an opponent. But after studying the teachings of Gandhi, he began to accept the ideas of nonviolence as well.

*Mohandas Gandhi
(1869-1948), often
called Mahatma
(or "great souled")
by his followers, used
peaceful resistance to
help India gain its
independence from
Great Britain
in 1947.*

As part of his preparation for the ministry, Young spent his summers traveling to different cities to preach and work in churches. In 1952, he went to work in a rural church near Marion, Alabama. There, he met a woman named Jean Childs, who was then a student at Manchester College in Indiana. The couple shared many of the same goals in life, and they were both religious people who wanted to help others.

In 1953, Young traveled to Austria to assist Eastern European refugees. When he returned to the United States, he married Jean Childs on June 7, 1954. They found a small apartment in Hartford, and he continued his studies at the seminary. In February 1955, he received a bachelor of divinity degree from Hartford Theological Seminary, and he and Jean decided to work with poor, rural communities in Georgia.

Soon afterward, the Youngs were giving many black people in the South the help they needed to live better lives. They would talk to them about their voting rights and encourage them to register to vote, although attempting to vote had proved dangerous for blacks in the South at that time. When Young became frustrated by the racism and bigotry that blacks continually had to endure in many southern towns, he accepted a position in New York City with the National Council of Churches.

Soon after moving to New York, however, both Andrew and Jean felt they had to return to the South, even though the work was frustrating. The couple and their three daughters, Andrea, Lisa, and Paula, settled in Atlanta, Georgia, where Young worked with Martin Luther King Jr. in the Southern Christian Leadership Conference (SCLC) and the Congress of Racial Equality (CORE). He became one of the strongest and ablest young leaders in the SCLC, and King relied on him to organize and plan major civil rights rallies and demonstrations for the organization.

Young was most effective at directing the nonviolent demonstrations during the 1963 Birmingham campaign, which brought the civil rights movement into the minds of all Americans. While watching the television news, Americans saw Birmingham Police chief "Bull" Conner's police dogs attack peaceful demonstrators in the streets, and firefighters spray people with hoses that were strong enough to knock down children.

Despite these actions, King told Young that responding to this violence with more violence would not solve the problems that black people faced. If blacks retaliated violently, King said, then angry whites would become even more hostile and would kill even more black

Martin Luther King Jr., a member of the Southern Christian Leadership Conference, became one of the most vocal and influential members of the civil rights movement.

people. To King, the options were clear. African Americans must stay nonviolent or risk becoming "nonexistent."

Later in 1963, Young planned and organized the March on Washington, joining King and more than 200,000 people who attended the famous demonstration. After King was assassinated in 1968, Andrew Young continued working with the SCLC, but soon said, "there just comes a time when any social movement has to come off the street and enter politics." Resigning his position as the executive vice president of the SCLC, Young ran for Congress in the Fifth Congressional District of Georgia.

He lost the race, but in 1972, with the help of both blacks and whites, Young ran for the same congressional seat again, and this time he won. With this victory, Andrew Young became the first African-American congressman from Georgia since the Reconstruction period that had followed the Civil War. That same year, another African American, Barbara Jordan, won a congressional seat in Texas. They were the first two African Americans elected to Congress in the South since the turn of the century.

Young used his political office to continue advancing the rights of all Americans. He soon learned that being a new representative in Congress was just like being a freshman in high school or college. He had to learn a lot about the procedures, including the unspoken rule for freshmen representatives: Be seen and not heard.

Representative Barbara Jordan, who served in the U.S. Congress from 1973 to 1979, received national attention in 1974 while investigating President Richard Nixon's involvement in the Watergate controversy.

In Congress, Young was assigned to the Banking and Currency Committee, where he felt unable to help poor people. He also found that getting a bill passed was extremely difficult. Despite the opposition he felt, Young realized that if he wanted to be reelected, he had to produce. His success would be based on how many bills he proposed in Congress, not necessarily how important those bills were. If he wanted to be reelected, he would have to sponsor legislation.

Meanwhile, the Young's fourth child, Andrew III, was born a month after he was sworn into office. The birth sent Andrew Young home often to Atlanta, where he spent time with his family and was able to remain close to his constituents, the people who had voted him into office. "I'm going to be a working representative," he told the people of Atlanta shortly after his election. He then went on to say the following:

That's how we won; we got out and worked. I try to tell these young people it's not always the good guy who wins the election, but the man who works harder. If the better man just happens to work a little harder, then he wins, but the bad guys are usually up early in the morning. I intend to visit my district every weekend. Church on Sundays. A school on Monday. That's doubly important where black people are concerned. We're terribly cynical about people we don't see. We don't read too much about our men in the paper. So it's their physical presence and accessibility that counts.

Young kept his promise to his constituents and voted only for bills that would help the people in his district. During his term, he continually voted against budget cuts proposed by President Richard Nixon's administration that would reduce the amount of money spent on welfare, health, housing, sewage treatment plants, and urban development. He supported legislation to increase the minimum wage and to improve public assistance benefits for the poor. His district in Georgia reelected him to Congress twice more—in 1974 and in 1976.

When he was appointed the U.S. ambassador to the United Nations during the presidency of Jimmy Carter, Young was presented with perhaps his best opportunity to influence the struggle for equality. As a cabinet member,

As U.S. ambassador to the United Nations, Andrew Young was not afraid to express controversial opinions and challenge the status quo. The United Nations building in New York City is pictured on the right.

he became the most important African American in President Carter's administration.

Young served as an ambassador from 1977 to 1979, and he was able to improve relations between the United States and the African and Caribbean nations in the areas of human rights and economic development. He left the United Nations after he had secretly met with members of the Palestine Liberation Organization (PLO), which the U.S. government regarded as a terrorist group. After Carter reprimanded Young, the ambassador resigned from his position because he could not guarantee that his views would not further embarrass the president.

In 1981, the citizens of Atlanta elected Young as their mayor, and they reelected him in 1985. He ran for governor of Georgia in 1990 but was defeated in the Democratic primary. Andrew Young's wife, Jean, died on September 16, 1994. Despite his grief, he continues to speak out against racism to audiences across the country.

Martin Luther King Jr. (1929-1968) inspired millions of people by speaking out against racial hatred and in favor of peaceful protest.

6

Martin Luther King Jr.
A Dreamer for a Nation

*A*s Martin Luther King Jr. stood at the top of the stairs of the Lincoln Memorial on August 28, 1963, more than 200,000 people looked up from the streets of Washington, D.C. Hot, tired, and crammed together, the crowd had already listened for hours to other speakers during the historic March on Washington—the emotional high point of the civil rights movement. When King began speaking, the crowd listened intently to his carefully prepared words as he delivered his now famous "I Have a Dream" speech:

Five score years ago, a great American in whose symbolic shadow we stand today, signed the Emancipation Proclamation. . . . But 100 years later, the Negro still is not free; 100 years later, the life of the Negro is still sadly crippled by the manacles of segregation and the chains of discrimination . . . . There will be neither rest nor tranquillity in America until the Negro is granted his citizenship rights. The whirlwind revolt will continue to shake the foundations of our nation until the bright day of justice emerges . . . . We cannot be satisfied as long as the Negro is the victim of the unspeakable horrors of police brutality . . . . We can never be satisfied as long as the Negro in Mississippi cannot vote and a Negro in New York believes he has nothing for which to vote.

Then, after a few minutes, King put his notes down and began speaking from his heart:

So I say to you today, my friends, that in spite of the difficulties and frustrations of the movement, I still have a dream. It is a dream deeply rooted in the American dream that one day this nation will rise up and live out the true meaning of its creed "we hold these truths to be self-evident, that all men are created equal."

On that day in August 1963, black people across the United States felt a strong sense of unity. Martin Luther King Jr. had become a national symbol for equality. By the time King delivered his speech, he had already waged a battle against racism for many years. During the 12

More than 200,000 people attended the March on Washington in 1963, an event that is often called the high point of the civil rights movement.

years of his career as a civil rights leader, he led one of the most important movements for social change in the twentieth century.

The man known as Martin Luther King Jr. had been named Michael Luther King when he was born on January 15, 1929, in Atlanta, Georgia, to Martin Luther King Sr., a Baptist minister, and Alberta Williams King, a teacher. In 1934, his father changed his son's name to Martin Luther King Jr.

Martin Jr. had an older sister, Willie, and a younger brother, Alfred. His grandmother, Jenny Williams, stayed with his family while he was growing up. The Kings lived near a family-owned grocery store, and young Martin often played with the white grocer's two sons. The three young children did nearly everything together. But one day when he went to play with his friends, their mother told him that her sons could never play with him again because he was black.

Hurt and crying, Martin ran home to tell his mother what had happened. This was his first experience with racial prejudice. His mother dried his tears and tried to explain how this hatred had begun. She told him how slave traders brought blacks from Africa to North America as early as the 1600s and sold them as slaves. She told him his grandfather had been a slave. She explained that although the Civil War had ended slavery, blacks were still not free because hatred and prejudice continued in the

United States. After consoling her son, she told Martin, "You are as good as anyone."

Before Martin began school, his mother taught him how to read. He studied books about great African-American leaders of the nineteenth-century, such as abolitionist Harriet Tubman, scientist George Washington Carver, and journalist Frederick Douglass. After learning about their accomplishments and disappointments, Martin concluded that blacks had to be twice as smart and twice as well-behaved as whites in order to be accepted into white society.

Martin Luther King Jr. watched his father preach on Sundays. He also had the opportunity to observe how his father handled racism. Once when they went shopping for a pair of shoes, the clerk told them to sit in the back of the store. His father told the clerk they would sit where they were or they would not buy any shoes in that store. The clerk still refused to help them near the front of the store, so his father decided to leave the store without the shoes as a matter of principle.

As a child, Martin Luther King Jr. watched blacks pay their bus fare in the front of the bus and then exit and re-enter through the back door. He watched as blacks sat in the back and then gave up their seats if whites asked for them.

In high school, King became an excellent student and a talented public speaker—a skill he would become known for as an adult. At age 15, he was admitted to

After escaping from slavery in 1849, Harriet Tubman (1820?-1913) helped more than 300 other slaves escape from their white owners in the South to northern states or into Canada.

George Washington Carver (1864?-1943), who served as director of agricultural research at Tuskegee Institute, helped to revive the southern economy by developing new uses for peanuts and other agricultural products.

Abolitionist Frederick Douglass (1817?-1895), who escaped from slavery in 1838 and spent several years in Europe, wrote harsh anti-slavery articles for 17 years in his North Star *newspaper, one of the first successful periodicals published by an African American.*

Morehouse College, a black school in his hometown. King initially wanted to be a medical doctor, then he changed his mind and considered becoming a lawyer. Finally, he decided to become a minister. King's father and Benjamin Mays, the president of Morehouse College, encouraged him in his decision. King preached his first sermon when he was 18.

After graduating from Morehouse, Martin continued his studies at Crozer Theological Seminary in Chester, Pennsylvania. This was the first time he attended a school with white students. There, he studied the life of philosopher Henry David Thoreau, whose 1849 essay "Civil Disobedience" supported nonviolent opposition to injustice.

Martin also learned about Mohandas Gandhi, a great philosopher from India. King admired Gandhi, who was fighting British rule in his country at this time without using guns or fists. Although the British shot and killed 400 of Gandhi's followers, Gandhi responded by calling for nonviolent protest. He went on hunger strikes, and his followers threw themselves across roads to stop traffic. In 1947, the people of India won their 30-year struggle for freedom from the British without fighting.

In June 1951, Martin graduated from Crozer at the top of his class. Later that year, he entered Boston University to study for his doctorate in theology. In 1952, King fell in love with a music student named Coretta Scott. Born in Marion, Alabama, Coretta also knew the hatred of racism. Her family's house had been burned down when she young, and Coretta became strong and determined in her fight against racism.

When Martin's parents met Coretta while visiting him in Boston, Martin Sr. implied that she was not good enough for his son. Coretta stood up to him, and he later agreed that Martin had made an excellent choice in deciding to marry her. Martin Luther King Sr. married Martin and Coretta on the Scott family's lawn in Alabama in 1953.

After graduating from Boston University, Martin had many choices about what to do with his career. He and Coretta decided they would return to the South, where King accepted a position as pastor of the Dexter Avenue Baptist Church in Montgomery, Alabama. Coretta was not anxious to go back to Alabama because she wanted to perform on stage, but she did like the idea of being closer to home. In Montgomery, Coretta gave birth to their first child, Yolanda. The Kings had three more children in the years that followed, Martin Luther King III, Bernice Albertine, and Dexter Scott.

In the early 1950s, black people in Montgomery were strongly held in the grips of "Jim Crow," a segregation system that required blacks and whites to live separately. Under the law, blacks and whites were supposed to be treated as equals—but they seldom were. On December 1, 1955, a tired black woman named Rosa Parks was riding in the middle of a bus, just behind the "whites only" sign. The bus became so crowded that the driver asked Parks and three other black people to give their seats to white riders. Parks refused. The driver stopped the bus and called the police. When the police arrived, they arrested Rosa Parks. (Although Rosa Parks received a great deal of publicity for refusing to give up her seat, many other black people had been arrested in previous months for doing the same thing.)

The morning after Rosa Parks's arrest, King received a call from E.D. Nixon, the president of the Alabama chapter of the National Association for the Advancement of Colored People (NAACP). Nixon was also the local organizer of the Brotherhood of Sleeping Car Porters, a union of black railroad workers who had requested help in organizing a one-day boycott of the Montgomery buses. The NAACP had been planning a boycott for months, and the incident of Rosa Parks's arrest became a catalyst for it. The African Americans in Birmingham used King's church as their meeting place as they planned the boycott.

Both King and his friend, the Reverend Ralph Abernathy, were on the committee to plan the boycott. In the coming years, the two men would march and protest together many times. The Sunday before the boycott began, black ministers spoke to the members of their congregations about Rosa Parks and asked them not to ride the buses. For most blacks, who represented about 70 percent of the city's riders, buses were their only means

Rosa Parks, who had joined the NAACP in 1943, is shown here in 1979, the year she received the organization's Springarn Medal for her "courage and determination" during the 1955 Montgomery bus boycott.

of transportation to their jobs. Boycotting the buses would mean a greater hardship for them than it would for most whites.

The boycott, which was to last until blacks could sit wherever they wished on the bus, began on December 5, 1955. Churches bought station wagons to take people to and from work. Blacks organized car pools and packed themselves into taxis. Thousands more walked long distances to work.

Soon, the police began arresting King and others for breaking "Jim Crow" segregation laws. To build dissension among the blacks in Montgomery, the whites spread lies about King, accusing him of opening a Swiss bank account with NAACP money. During this time, King received from 30 to 40 hate letters a day and about that many telephone calls from angry citizens. Sometimes the only sound he or his family heard when one of them answered the telephone was the sound of someone spitting into the receiver. Many angry callers threatened his life. "Listen, nigger," one said. "We've taken all we want from you; before next week you'll be sorry you ever came to Montgomery."

Understandably afraid of all the threats, King wanted to quit as a leader of the bus boycott. Feeling alone, he began to pray. He thought God was telling him to stand up for righteousness and for the truth. He believed that God was on his side.

Martin Luther King Jr. and other activists plan the Montgomery bus boycott, which lasted for over a year.

A few days later, the Kings' house was firebombed. Coretta and daughter Yolanda had been in the back and were unharmed. When an angry black crowd gathered outside his house, he calmed them by preaching what he had learned from Gandhi: "We must meet violence with nonviolence. . . . We must love our white brothers. . . . We must meet hate with love."

About one year after the boycott began, the U.S. Supreme Court ruled as unconstitutional the "Jim Crow" laws requiring blacks to ride in the back of a bus and give up their seats to whites. On December 21, 1956, King was pleasantly greeted by a white driver as he entered a bus to end the boycott. For more than a year, the black citizens of Montgomery had refused to ride the buses. Daily they had sacrificed to maintain this boycott, and they had finally won!

During these years, other groups were also involved in the struggle for civil rights in the United States. Two organizations—the National Urban League and the Congress of Racial Equality (CORE), were working for African Americans in northern cities. Since the battles fought by the NAACP up to this time had primarily been in northern courtrooms, the organization decided that another group should be formed to work exclusively in the South.

Because black ministers were considered to be influential leaders in their communities, these organizations encouraged southern ministers to unite. Soon, a group of

100

ministers started the Southern Christian Leadership Conference (SCLC). At a conference on February 14, 1957, they chose King—their most famous member—as the leader.

King's courage and fame had spread beyond the United States. Even Kwame Nkrumah, the prime minister of Ghana in West Africa, had heard about the civil rights leader. Ghana had just won its independence from Britain, and Nkrumah invited the King family to attend the celebrations in Ghana in March 1957. During this trip to Africa, the Kings also visited Nigeria, another West African nation still controlled by Britain. The poverty and suffering there, which was even worse than in the rural areas of the southern United States, shocked the King family.

When the family returned home, King began promoting his book about the Montgomery bus boycott, *Stride Toward Freedom: The Montgomery Story*. In September 1958, while autographing his book in a New York City department store, a well-dressed black woman stabbed him with a letter opener. Surgeons later had to remove one of his ribs and part of his breastbone to recover the instrument, which was pressing against the aorta of his heart. The letter opener had almost pierced the main artery of King' heart, which would have killed him.

During the enforced rest period that followed the attack, King and his wife traveled to India so he could learn more about Gandhi's principles of nonviolent resistance. When he returned to the United States, King decided to do something about the lack of voting rights for his people. About 5 million African Americans were eligible to vote, but only about 1.3 million were registered to vote. The SCLC filed complaints about voter registration with the newly formed Civil Rights Commission. King also used the SCLC to start programs to teach black people how to live nonviolently. To further the programs, he moved back to Atlanta, where the SCLC was based.

About this time, students in Greensboro, North Carolina, were holding sit-ins to desegregate all-white lunch counters. King helped the students by joining a sit-in at an Atlanta department store lunch counter. Soon sit-ins were taking place throughout the South.

In 1961, King supported the "freedom rides" that blacks and whites took in buses throughout the South. While on these journeys, the freedom riders sat at "whites-only" lunch counters, waited in "whites-only" areas at bus stations, and used restrooms designated for whites. Because of this, whites beat and kicked the freedom riders in Rock Hill, South Carolina, and in Birmingham, Alabama. In Anniston, Alabama, whites firebombed one bus. When King led a protest march in Birmingham, the police turned fire hoses and dogs on the marchers. The police then jailed King and thousands of his followers.

Black and white students at the University of Missouri protest segregation policies by sitting together at lunch.

After King gave the "I Have A Dream" speech during the March on Washington, *Time* magazine named him "Man of the Year" for 1963. In 1964, King became the fourteenth U.S. citizen and the second African American to win the Nobel Peace Prize. (At age 35, he was the youngest person ever to win the prize.) He divided the $54,000 that came with the award among several civil rights groups.

The Nobel Peace Prize filled King with joy and motivation to continue on in his struggle against racism and segregation. But his workdays were long and he was tired. By October 1964, he had given about 350 civil rights speeches and had traveled more than 275,000 miles. He continued preaching at Ebenezer Baptist Church, although his pulpit had spread far beyond the doors of the Atlanta-based church.

During the early 1960s, King also led a voter registration protest in Selma, Alabama, which eventually led to a 50-mile march from Selma to Montgomery. He met with President Lyndon Johnson, who supported the Civil Rights Act of 1964 and the Voting Rights Act of 1965. These acts of Congress led to the removal of the "whites-only" signs in southern restaurants, restrooms, and bus and train stations and prohibited unfair literacy tests designed to prevent blacks from voting. "Jim Crow" was being run out of the country!

Despite King's call for nonviolence, violence erupted all around him. While freedom workers were being beaten and killed, blacks were rioting, smashing, and burning the northern cities in which they lived. Although the movement that King led remained peaceful, much of the protest around the United States turned violent.

In 1966, King moved his family and the SCLC headquarters to Chicago, where they found poverty instead of "Jim Crow" laws. King planned to attack poverty by organizing a Poor People's March on Washington. On April 4, 1968, a few days before the march was to take place, King went to Memphis, Tennessee, to help lead a protest for equal pay among garbage workers. As he leaned over the railing on the balcony outside of his second-floor room at the Lorraine Motel, he was fatally shot. King was 39.

The police charged a white man named James Earl Ray with King's murder. They accused Ray of firing the fatal shot while standing in an empty bathtub in a house across the street from the motel. Thousands of people mourned King's death, and Coretta Scott King led a march that became a memorial to her husband. She then flew his body back to Atlanta, where as many as 100,000 people surrounded Ebenezer Baptist Church for his funeral. He was originally buried in the city's Southview Cemetery, but his body was later moved to the grounds of

In April 1968, mourners across the country marched to honor the memory of Martin Luther King Jr.

Furious over Martin Luther King's assassination, some people resorted to looting and riots—actions that angered many of his supporters.

the Martin Luther King Center for Nonviolent Change, also in Atlanta.

King, who had become a champion for his people, is still remembered today as a great leader who brought needed change to his country. His accomplishments are celebrated each year on the third Monday of January.

Martin Luther King Jr. gave his life for his dream of freedom, equality, and peace. At his burial, his friend, Ralph Abernathy, said, "The cemetery is too small for his spirit, but we submit his body to the ground. The grave is too narrow for his soul but we commit his body to the ground. No coffin, no crypt, no stone can hold his greatness. But we submit his body to the ground."

Inscribed on a marker at King's gravesite in Atlanta are the following words from his famous "I Have a Dream" speech: "Free At Last, Free At Last. Thank God Almighty, I'm Free At Last."

In the nearly 30 years following her husband's death, Coretta Scott King and her children have remained involved in civil rights activities.

Malcolm X (1925-1965), who described himself as the "angriest man in America," told blacks to stand up for their rights and defend themselves against racist attacks.

7

Malcolm X
A Leader of Black Pride

*O*f all the civil rights leaders of the twentieth century, Malcolm X probably led the most controversial life. After leaving a group of Black Muslims, known as the Nation of Islam, he set out to build a new movement for black liberation. A confident man and excellent public speaker, Malcolm X was a charismatic leader. His thousands of followers were tired of existing conditions and wanted to change the way black people were treated in the United States.

During his life, and for many years after his death, most people thought of Malcolm X only as the young minister for the Nation of Islam who openly called white people "devils" and said whites were naturally evil. In televised interviews, Malcolm X often called himself "the angriest man in America." But many people today also remember his teachings about racial pride and the contributions of black people throughout history.

The future civil rights leader was born Malcolm Little on May 19, 1925, in Omaha, Nebraska, to Louise Little and the Reverend Earl Little, a Baptist minister. His father had three children by a previous marriage (Ella, Earl, and Mary, who lived in Boston) and six children in his second marriage (Wilfred, Hilda, Philbert, Malcolm, Reginald, and Yvonne).

Shortly after Malcolm was born, the Little family moved to Milwaukee, Wisconsin, because the Ku Klux Klan was threatening Reverend Little. The Klan did not like Little because he was an organizer for Marcus Garvey's Universal Negro Improvement Association (UNIA). Little was helping Garvey to promote black race purity and black pride. Garvey advised black people to return to their ancestral homeland in Africa. Malcolm's father accepted Garvey's teachings because he believed that black people could never achieve freedom, independence, and self respect in the United States.

Malcolm's father had reasons for his beliefs. Four of his six brothers died violently. White men had killed

*Marcus Garvey
(1887-1940) founded
the Universal Negro
Improvement Association
in 1914 to promote racial
pride among blacks.
Millions of black people
supported his "back to
Africa" movement, but
Garvey lost support after
misusing the
organization's funds
during the 1920s.*

*Originally intended to restore pride to the South after
the Civil War, the Ku Klux Klan has been responsible
for hundreds of acts of violence against African
Americans since the organization began in 1865.*

three of them, including Malcolm's uncle Oscar, who was shot by a white police officer. Because of these stories about his uncles, Malcolm grew up worrying that he, too, would die a violent death. He spent his youth preparing himself for death.

The Little family lived in Milwaukee for only a short time. (Malcolm's younger brother, Reginald, was born there.) After that, they moved to Lansing, Michigan, where his sister, Yvonne, was born. There, a hate group called the Black Legion threatened the family. The members of the Legion did not like Malcolm's father because he had bought a house outside the black area and he often talked about blacks returning to Africa. Some black people in the community told white people lies about Little to cause whites to hate him even more. Four-year-old Malcolm experienced his first racially motivated attack when men with guns set the Little house on fire. When the family moved to East Lansing, they were again harassed by whites. Finally, they settled in a four-room house his father built in the country, two miles outside of town.

In 1931, Malcolm's father died from a beating by unknown assailants who were never found. Malcolm's mother, who was then 34, was left to raise her children. Because she was not able single-handedly to provide for her children, the family went on welfare. The family's situation became even worse in 1934, in the middle of the Great Depression. Malcolm and his brothers shot rabbits, trapped muskrats, and speared frogs. They then earned money by selling these animals—but there still wasn't enough to support the family. Feeling deprived and hungry, Malcolm began stealing apples and other treats from stores.

Malcolm's mother and the welfare workers who visited the Little home began to worry more about Malcolm than the other children. His mother eventually had a nervous breakdown and was committed to a mental hospital. At age 13, Malcolm was placed in a foster home. Soon afterward, he was sent to a juvenile state detention ward because of his bad behavior. As a state ward, Malcolm began to do well in school. Even though many of the white students and teachers regularly called him a "nigger," he still became popular. Elected class president, he was ranked as one of the top three students of his seventh grade class.

During the summer between seventh and eighth grades, Malcolm lived with his stepsister, Ella, in Boston. After finishing eighth grade, Malcolm moved to Boston, where he decided to work rather than return to school. Ella encouraged him to get to know people in the better parts of Boston, but he was more attracted to the city's ghetto. There he met his friend, Shorty, who showed him how to straighten his hair in a style called a "conk."

Malcolm soon began copying the sharply dressed men who hung around the pool rooms, bars, and restaurants trying to hustle money. One of his first jobs was as a shoe shiner at the Roseland State Ballroom. As he supplemented his income by selling marijuana, Malcolm's love for the underworld grew.

In 1942, Malcolm moved to New York City, where he joined the black community's underworld of hustling and stealing. His street name was Detroit Red. While staying high on marijuana, opium, and Benzedrine, he soon turned to armed robbery. Scrapes with other hustlers sent him fleeing back to Boston, where his criminal ways finally caught up with him. Connected to a burglary in 1946, Malcolm was sentenced to ten years in prison.

In prison, Malcolm smoked cigarettes and marijuana that guards smuggled inside. He had a bad temper and would drop his tray on the floor of the prison dining hall and refused to answer to his prison number. He cursed so much his cellmates called him Satan. Another inmate, Bimbi, began talking to Malcolm about religion and education. As he listened, Malcolm discovered that his reading and writing skills were rusty because he had not used them very much since dropping out of school. His sisters encouraged him to study, and after a year he could once more compose well-written letters.

In 1948, he received a letter from his older brother, Philbert, saying he had discovered the "natural religion for the black man." Reginald and Hilda also wrote Malcolm and told him to accept *Allah*, the Muslim name for God, and Elijah Muhammad, the leader of the Nation of Islam. Members of this group, called Black Muslims,

*Spiritual leader Elijah Muhammad (1897-1975),
who claimed to be a messenger from God, inspired
many African Americans to follow his strict teachings
and join the Nation of Islam.*

sought to instill racial pride and promote self-sufficiency
among black people. The Muslim religion offered them
discipline and gave meaning to their lives. Reginald also
urged Malcolm to give up eating pork and smoking
cigarettes.

As his prison term wore on, Malcolm began to read
books from the prison library. Reginald and many of his
relatives continued writing and visiting him to talk about
Allah. As he thought about the white people in his life —

from his school teachers to the men who had killed his father and uncles—Malcolm came to believe that white people were devils.

Soon Malcolm began writing letters to Elijah Muhammad. Muhammad, who lived in Chicago, wrote back and welcomed Malcolm into the sect. Muhammad also replaced Malcolm's surname—Little—with the letter X. (Black Muslims changed their last names because these names had been given to their ancestors by white slave owners.) Through his letter writing and reading, Malcolm X began educating himself. He studied the dictionary, copying each page. With his increased vocabulary and his passion for learning, he began to understand more fully the books he was reading. By spending his time reading, the months in prison seemed to pass more quickly.

As he learned more, Malcolm X recognized the parallels between the teachings of Elijah Muhammad and the social activism of his father. Malcolm X learned that Elijah Muhammad had been sent to prison on a draft-dodging charge and had been sentenced to serve five years. The state had paroled Muhammad in 1946.

Malcolm X was paroled from prison in 1952. Not long afterward, he set out on a mission to use the teachings of the Nation of Islam to "stir and wake and resurrect the black man." Attacking long-standing racial attitudes in the United States, he recruited new members in the places he used to hang out—pool halls, bars, street corners. Speaking in both plain language and slang, he attracted the attention of many people.

As a reward for his hard work, Malcolm X was appointed head of Temple Number Seven in Harlem. Membership grew very quickly, and Malcolm set out across the country, organizing more temples along the East and West Coasts and converting more educated and affluent members. Malcolm X helped to increase membership in the Nation of Islam from 400 to 400,000. He traveled across the United States, teaching black people about the history of slavery. He told people how slaves had been forced to pull plows like horses and how they were sold from one plantation to another—the way farmers might sell chickens or cows to each other.

More importantly, Malcolm X told African Americans that their ancestors had been more than cotton-pickers. There had been many great black leaders, including Nat Turner (a slave who led a major revolt against white owners in 1831), François Dominique Toussaint L'Ouverture (an eighteenth-century Haitian who also rebelled against slavery), and Hannibal, a military genius from northern Africa who lived around 200 B.C. Malcolm X preached that when black people in the United States knew who they were, where they had come from, and what they had once been, they would begin to wonder who took away their memorable history. With those questions in their minds, African

Americans would then take action to get back their black heritage "by any means necessary." Because of the subject matter of Malcolm X's preaching, whites in the United States viewed him as a potentially dangerous man.

Around this time, Malcolm met his future wife, Betty Shabazz, at Temple Number Seven. The couple married in January 1958, and she changed her name to Betty X. Between November 1958 and the early 1960s, they had six children, Attallah, Qubilah, Ilyasah, Gamilah, Malaak, and Malikah.

In 1964, after eating and praying with Muslims of all races who had gathered from many countries in the holy cities of Mecca and Medina in Saudi Arabia, he gave up his racist views. He no longer believed white people were devils and accepted them as human beings. Now, when he condemned individual white people, it would be because of their actions, not their color. He also came to believe that whites could help the civil rights movement.

During this time, Martin Luther King Jr. and other civil rights leaders were challenging racism in the South by holding nonviolent boycotts and protests. Malcolm X thought that these protests were ludicrous. He said that King's nonviolent efforts were accomplishing "too little, too late" and that blacks should use active self-defense to fight off attacks by white racists. This meant that, while black people should not instigate violence, they should use violence to protect themselves if someone was physically attacking them. King, on the other hand, thought that people should *never* fight back, even if they were being assaulted.

Malcolm X also charged that Christian teachings and Mohandas Gandhi's principles of nonviolence were destructive because they taught black people not to fight back when whites lynched them, burned down their homes, or threw them into jail unjustly. Malcolm X told his listeners they could no longer afford to wait for racial justice to be won:

> Who's going to wait for years? . . . Why should he wait for what other people have when they're born? Why should he have to go to a Supreme Court or to a Congress, or to a Senate, or to some kind of legislative body to be told he's a man when other people don't have to go through that process to be told they're a man?

In the early 1960s, Malcolm X and the Nation of Islam had become well known to both blacks and whites throughout the United States. Critics called Malcolm a hatemonger who preached violence and destruction. He responded by saying that only radical tactics would get results.

By 1962, Elijah Muhammad had grown ill, and he asked Malcolm X to serve as his spokesman in public. These public appearances made other Black Muslims jealous, and they began to spread rumors that Malcolm X was trying to take over their group. Before long, a political fight developed between Malcolm X and Elijah Muhammad.

The bad feelings between the two leaders worsened when President John F. Kennedy was assassinated in November 1963. Malcolm X had previously criticized the Kennedy administration for not doing enough to stop racist activities by the Ku Klux Klan. After Kennedy's assassination, Malcolm X said during a speech that the "chickens [have] come home to roost." His words implied that whites were being repaid for creating a climate of violence in the country. The statement outraged whites, and concerned Elijah Muhammad, who suspended Malcolm X from his duties for 90 days. During this time,

John F. Kennedy (1917-1963), who served as U.S. president from 1961 until his death, was one of several prominent public figures who were assassinated during the 1960s.

Muhammad learned that a high-ranking Black Muslim had ordered Malcolm X to be assassinated. Louis Farrakhan, whom Malcolm X had once mentored, stated that Malcolm X was a traitor to the Nation of Islam and deserved to die.

In the midst of this controversy, in March 1964, Malcolm X announced that he had decided to leave the Nation of Islam to form Muslim Mosque, Incorporated. Less than a month later, he made a pilgrimage to Saudi Arabia and formed a nonreligious branch of Muslim Mosque called the Organization of Afro-American Unity (OAAU). These efforts to establish racial equality and to end white supremacy drew more death threats. Malcolm suspected that Black Muslims who disagreed with his philosophies were behind these threats.

Malcolm X and his family barely managed to escape their Elmhurst, New York, home alive when it was fire-bombed on February 14, 1965. Several days later, he spoke to a crowd of 400 people at the Audubon Ballroom in Harlem. During his speech on February 21, three gunmen—allegedly Black Muslims—created a disturbance and fatally shot him. Police caught one of them, Talmadge Hayer, but the other two escaped and were never caught. Two days later, someone set Malcolm X's New York City headquarters afire and it burned to the ground.

During the early 1960s, Malcolm X had told his life story to the African-American writer Alex Haley, who

Although Malcolm X was considered to be highly controversial during his lifetime, many Americans—both black and white—now regard him as a role model.

wrote *The Autobiography of Malcolm X* in 1964. After reading the book, whites could understand how Malcolm X had come to hate them. Except for a few speeches and his book, *Malcolm X Speaks*, Malcolm X had few opportunities to display his new vision of racial cooperation and the use of violence only in self-defense.

Nearly 30 years after his death, the teachings of Malcolm X are still alive. His life was most recently celebrated through the highly successful 1992 motion picture *Malcolm X*, which was produced by Spike Lee. Although Malcolm X was considered dangerous by many people during his lifetime, others felt sympathetic toward him after his death.

In 1968, Shirley Chisholm became the first black woman elected to the U.S. House of Representatives. Four years later, she was the first black person—male or female—to run for president of the United States.

8

Other Notable African-American Civil Rights Leaders

*M*any people see the assassinations of Martin Luther King Jr. and Malcolm X during the 1960s as the end of the civil rights movement. Although their deaths both saddened and angered people throughout the United States, African Americans have continued to work for increased rights and opportunities over the past 30 years.

One of them was Shirley Chisholm, who sought the Democratic nomination for U.S. president in 1972. Inspired by black role models such as nineteenth-century journalist Ida B. Wells and twentieth-century educator

Mary McLeod Bethune, Chisholm believed there was no reason to leave politics to men.

Chisholm, the nation's first black congresswoman, was born Shirley Anita St. Hill on November 30, 1924, in Brooklyn, New York. Her family stressed the value of education. Shirley graduated from high school at the top of her class and received college scholarship offers from Vassar and Oberlin. But because she did not have enough money to leave home to go to school even with a

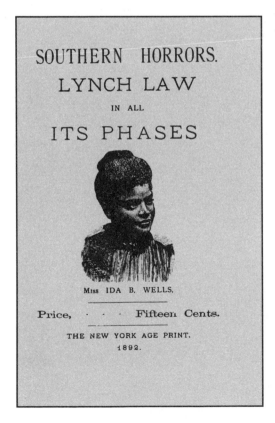

In her newspaper columns, editor Ida B. Wells (1862-1931) wrote about the violence against blacks that was especially prevalent in the decades following the Civil War.

Mary McLeod Bethune (center in hat) founded the National Council of Negro Women in 1935. Bethune (1875-1955) also worked as an adviser of minority affairs for President Franklin D. Roosevelt.

scholarship, she remained in New York City and attended Brooklyn College.

When Chisholm graduated from college with honors in 1946, some of her professors urged her to consider a career in politics. However, she initially thought this dream would be impossible to achieve because she was both black and a woman. Nevertheless, she decided to enter politics in 1960. Wanting to replace the traditional political party in her district with a new, liberal party, Chisholm and others formed the Unity Democratic Club. In 1962, two of the organization's candidates won seats in the New York State Assembly.

With this win, the Unity Democratic Club gained political control of the district. In 1964, when one of the assemblymen left to become a judge, Chisholm decided she would run for the vacant state legislative seat. That fall, she won in a landslide victory.

Chisholm went to Albany, New York, and served as assemblywoman for the Seventeenth District from 1964 to 1968. Chisholm proved to be a tough politician, and she was able to get bills passed that provided college funds for students and established an unemployment insurance fund for domestic workers.

Chisholm next turned to national politics. A redistricting of her residential area created the Twelfth Congressional District, which turned out to be predominately black. In her race for the congressional seat, Chisholm beat the Republican candidate, James Farmer, one of the founders of the Congress of Racial Equality (CORE).

In 1969, Chisholm took her place as the first African-American woman to become a member of the House of Representatives. She quickly decided that she could help people of color more by running for president, and in 1972 she became the first black person to run for the country's highest office.

Although Chisholm lost the Democratic nomination to South Dakota senator George McGovern, her quest led the way for other women and for blacks to run for high office. After the election, Chisholm told reporters that her defeat was a triumph:

*Shirley Chisholm—
as an African
American and as a
woman—ran her
political campaigns
as an outsider.*

In terms of black politics, I think an effect of my campaign has been to increase the independence and self-reliance of many local elected black officials and black political activists from the domination of the political "superstars." . . . Who can tell? What I hope most is that now there will be others who will feel themselves as capable of running for high political office as any wealthy, good-looking white male.

Chisholm was right. Another black activist, Jesse Jackson, campaigned for president in 1984 and 1988. As a political leader, Jackson ran on a diverse and multicultural platform backed by his organization, the National Rainbow Coalition. Although he was not elected,

Jesse Jackson won many supporters while campaigning during the 1984 and 1988 presidential primaries.

Jackson's strong support in several northern and southern states proved that his campaign for the presidency was more than symbolic.

Earlier in his career, Jackson had worked with Martin Luther King Jr. In 1967, King appointed him to head Operation Breadbasket, the economic section of the Southern Christian Leadership Conference (SCLC). The organization, a coalition of business leaders and ministers, cooperated with white-owned companies to create job opportunities for blacks. In 1968, Jackson was ordained a Baptist minister.

After leaving Operation Breadbasket in 1971, Jackson founded People United to Save Humanity (PUSH) and became the group's executive director. From Chicago, he expanded the organization to 14 major cities. Operation PUSH led to national agreements with large corporations such as Kentucky Fried Chicken and Burger King to provide more jobs for African Americans.

In the years since his 1988 bid for the presidency, Jackson has remained on the world stage. In 1989, Jackson moved his family to Washington, D.C. The following year he became a non-voting "shadow senator" for the District of Columbia, a symbolic post the city government had created with the hope of turning the district into the 51st U.S. state.

During the Persian Gulf War of 1991, which began after the Iraqi invasion of Kuwait, Jackson negotiated for the release of about 300 political hostages—citizens of the United States and other countries—who were being held captive in Iraq. His success embarrassed U.S. president George Bush and other chiefs of state, who had been unable to persuade Iraqi leader Saddam Hussein to release the hostages. Jackson also became the host of a nationally syndicated Washington, D.C., talk show that informed the public about important issues affecting African Americans.

In 1991, President Bush was faced with the responsibility of filling the vacancy left open on the Supreme Court when liberal Justice Thurgood Marshall retired. In July 1991, Bush nominated Court of Appeals judge Clarence Thomas, who appeared to be the ideological opposite of Marshall, to fill that position. The nationally televised Senate confirmation hearings in October 1991 became hostile when a black law professor, Anita Hill, accused Thomas of making sexual advances toward her years earlier when he had been her supervisor at the Equal Employment Opportunity Commission in Washington, D.C. Despite the controversy, the Senate confirmed Thomas by a 52 to 48 vote.

Thomas, who had been born in Pin Point, Georgia, on June 23, 1948, became the 106th Supreme Court justice and the second African-American justice to serve on the Court.

While many African Americans were upset by Justice Thomas's conservative legal views, his appointment to the nation's highest court reflected the diversity

Although some were disappointed that conservative judge Clarence Thomas filled the Supreme Court seat left open by Thurgood Marshall, many black Americans were still pleased to have another African American on the high court.

of beliefs within the African-American community, demonstrating that black people are not homogenous in their thinking.

Another prominent African-American, civil rights scholar Lani Guinier, received harsh public scrutiny when President Bill Clinton nominated her to the position of assistant attorney general of civil rights in April 1993. Before Guinier, a law professor at the University of Pennsylvania, could discuss her beliefs and qualifications, a host of people were calling for Clinton to withdraw his nomination. After reading only a small portion of her legal writings, conservative opponents called her "Quota Queen," claiming she would force businesses and schools

133

to recruit large numbers of minority applicants even if they weren't qualified.

On June 3, 1993, President Clinton said he had reread Guinier's writings and was withdrawing her nomination because he disagreed with her views on democratic fairness. In 1994, Guinier published her legal briefs in a book entitled *The Tyranny of the Majority*, in which she discussed many of her views that hadn't been publicly known at the time of her nomination. She believed that many Americans have given up their right to vote because they do not think their vote means anything if their candidate fails to win. Even if the candidate they supported doesn't win, Guinier wrote, their votes are important because they will encourage other candidates with similar views to run in the future.

Carol Moseley Braun, the first African-American woman to serve as a U.S. senator, surprised much of the nation when she was elected to the U.S. Senate in November 1992. Born on August 16, 1947, in Chicago, Moseley Braun began her national political career when she was elected to the Illinois House of Representatives in 1978 at the age of 31. Committed to responsible government, Moseley Braun had a successful decade working in the state legislature, and she became a vocal supporter of laws that help women and minorities.

Marian Wright Edelman, a veteran of the civil rights movement and a former attorney for the National Association for the Advancement of Colored People, has

In 1992, Carol Moseley Braun of Illinois became the first African-American woman elected to the U.S. Senate. She became a member of several Senate committees, including the judiciary committee, which reviews Supreme Court nominations.

spent much of her career trying to increase opportunities for young people. Winning a grant from the Field Foundation, she moved to Washington, D.C., in 1968 and established the Washington Research Project—the predecessor of the Children's Defense Fund, which was founded in 1973.

Edelman, who is often called "the children's crusader," became concerned about teenage pregnancy when she learned that 55.5 percent of black children in the United States were born out of wedlock and often to teenage mothers. Since then, she has brought an increased awareness to the problems facing children in the United States. Edelman has written several books, including the 1992 best-seller *The Measure of Our Success: A Letter to My Children and Yours*. Using plain, easy-to-understand language, she explained what every American needs to do for the welfare of our children:

> Every morning, as we wake up, 100,000 American children wake up homeless. Every 13 seconds, as we get out of bed, an American child is reported abused or neglected. Every 32 seconds, about the time it takes us to walk to the kitchen and put on the coffee, an American baby is born into poverty. Every 14 minutes, while we shower and brush our teeth, a baby dies in America. Every 64 seconds, while we lock our doors and head for work, a baby is born to a teenage mother. And every 13 hours, before we go back to sleep at night, an American preschooler is murdered.

Edelman has repeatedly said that *all* American children deserve to have these three things: a healthy start (basic health care for children and pregnant women), a head start (good preschool and child care), and a fair start (job opportunities so parents can provide for their children, tax credits for families with children, and child support from absent parents). She believes that today's activists must continue working to improve these areas for future generations.

Important Events in African-American History

AUGUST 1619

A Dutch ship docks at Jamestown, Virginia, with 20 captured black Africans who are sold as servants shortly after their arrival.

1641

The North American colonies recognize Negro slavery as a legal institution.

1688

The Society of Friends (or Quakers) becomes the first organization in North America to adopt a formal anti-slavery resolution.

SEPTEMBER 9, 1739

The first major colonial slave uprising occurs in South Carolina.

JULY 2, 1777

Vermont becomes the first colony to abolish slavery.

1787

The U.S. Constitution is signed. Stating that blacks should be counted as only three-fifths of a person, for purposes of representation in Congress, the document becomes a source of tension for decades to come.

1808

The legal U.S. slave trade ends, but slavery continues within the new nation.

1830

More than 2 million slaves live in the United States.

During the early 1800s, many slaves tried to escape from their white owners in the South, often fleeing to northern states or as far away as Canada.

AUGUST 21-22, 1831

Nat Turner leads a massive slave revolt in Virginia, called the "Southampton Insurrection," and 60 slaves kill 55 white people.

MARCH 20, 1852

Harriet Beecher Stowe writes *Uncle Tom's Cabin*, a book about North American slaves.

JANUARY 1, 1854

The first black college, the Lincoln Institute, is chartered at Jefferson City, Missouri.

In *Dred Scott v. Sanford*, the U.S. Supreme Court declares that blacks are not legal citizens of the United States and denies Congress any power to prohibit slavery.

President Abraham Lincoln signs the Emancipation Proclamation, officially making slavery an issue in the Civil War. More than 186,000 blacks fought for the North during the war, which began in 1861 and ended in 1865.

Despite fighting for the Union during the Civil War, black soldiers received inferior wages, food, and benefits compared to their white counterparts.

1865

The Thirteenth Amendment to the U.S. Constitution outlaws slavery.

1868

The Fourteenth Amendment states that everyone born or naturalized in the United States is a U.S. citizen.

FEBRUARY 23, 1868

William Edward Burghardt Du Bois is born in Great Barrington, Massachusetts.

1870

The Fifteenth Amendment states that people cannot be stopped from voting because of race, color, or previous servitude.

MAY 18, 1896

In *Plessy v. Ferguson*, the U.S. Supreme Court approves the doctrine of "separate but equal," which leads to "Jim Crow" segregation laws in the South for 60 years.

1900

The Pan-African movement convenes in London, England, demanding the union of all Africans and the elimination of colonialism and white supremacy.

DECEMBER 13, 1903

Ella Baker is born in Norfolk, Virginia.

JULY 11-13, 1905

A group of Negro leaders meets on the Canadian side of Niagara Falls, which leads to the formation of the Niagara Movement.

JULY 2, 1908

Thurgood Marshall is born in Baltimore, Maryland.

140

Segregated theaters, like this one, were common throughout the South during the first half of the twentieth century.

FEBRUARY 12, 1909

The National Association for the Advancement of Colored People (NAACP), the oldest existing Negro organization in America, holds its first conference in New York City. It is officially founded the following year.

APRIL 1910

An organization to assist black city dwellers, the National Urban League, is created.

JANUARY 12, 1920

James Farmer, leader of CORE, is born in Marshall, Texas.

MAY 19, 1925

Malcolm X is born as Malcolm Little in Omaha, Nebraska.

JANUARY 15, 1929

Martin Luther King Jr. is born in Atlanta, Georgia.

MARCH 12, 1932

Andrew Young is born in New Orleans, Louisiana.

1942

The Committee of Racial Equality (CORE) is established to promote interracial, nonviolent direct action against racial segregation.

1944

With growing numbers, CORE changes its name to the Congress of Racial Equality.

1950

Ralph Bunche becomes the first African American to win a Nobel Peace Prize, for his work to end hostilities between Israel and Arab countries the previous year.

MAY 17, 1954

The Supreme Court's decision in *Brown v. The Board of Education of Topeka* makes racial segregation in public schools illegal.

DECEMBER 5, 1955

Four days after Rosa Parks's arrest, Martin Luther King Jr. begins leading the year-long Montgomery, Alabama, bus boycott, protesting civil inequalities.

NOVEMBER 15, 1956

The U.S. Supreme Court declares that "Jim Crow" segregation laws are unconstitutional.

DECEMBER 21, 1956

After more than a year, the Montgomery bus boycott ends, and whites and blacks no longer ride separately on city buses.

FEBRUARY 14, 1957

Martin Luther King Jr. and other activists form the Southern Christian Leadership Conference (SCLC) to oppose racial discrimination in the South.

AUGUST 29, 1957

The Voting Rights Act of 1957, the first major civil rights legislation since 1875, is passed.

SEPTEMBER 24-25, 1957

Federal troops oppose Arkansas governor Orval Faubus in his attempt to block desegregation of public schools in Little Rock.

FEBRUARY 12, 1958

The Crusade for Citizenship, an effort to register black voters, is launched in the South.

*Black and white college students often held nonviolent
sit-ins during the 1960s to oppose racial segregation.*

FEBRUARY 1, 1960

The first "sit-ins" at segregated lunch counters begin a wave of similar, nonviolent, protests across the South.

APRIL 15-17, 1960

The Student Nonviolent Coordinating Committee (SNCC) is founded in Raleigh, North Carolina.

APRIL 3, 1963

Birmingham, Alabama, protesters and children are sprayed by high-powered hoses and attacked by police dogs.

AUGUST 27, 1963

W.E.B. Du Bois dies at age 95.

AUGUST 28, 1963

During the March on Washington, 200,000 people gather at the Lincoln Memorial and hear civil rights leaders speak. Martin Luther King Jr. gives his famous "I Have a Dream" speech.

1964

The Civil Rights Act of 1964 outlaws racial discrimination in public facilities.

During "Freedom Summer," blacks and whites protest interstate bus segregation as "freedom riders" travel across the South.

DECEMBER 10, 1964

Martin Luther King Jr. is awarded the Nobel Peace Prize in Oslo, Norway.

1965

The Voting Rights Act of 1965 outlaws literacy tests and other practices designed to prevent people from being allowed to vote.

FEBRUARY 21, 1965

Malcolm X is assassinated at the Audubon Ballroom in Harlem, New York.

AUGUST 11-21, 1965

The Watts Riots leave 34 dead, 900 injured, 3500 arrested, and $225 million in property damage in a clash between blacks and white police officers in Los Angeles, California.

1966

The militant Black Panther Party is established.

Robert Weaver is appointed secretary of the U.S. Housing and Urban Development Department, the first black in a U.S. Cabinet.

1967

Thurgood Marshall becomes the first African American appointed to the U.S. Supreme Court.

APRIL 4, 1968

Martin Luther King Jr. is assassinated in Memphis, Tennessee, spawning massive riots in 125 cities.

1968

Shirley Chisholm is the first black woman elected to the U.S. House of Representatives.

1971

The U.S. Supreme Court upholds busing for desegregation.

1972

Shirley Chisholm is the first African American to run for president.

Barbara Jordan of Texas and Andrew Young of Georgia win seats in the U.S. House of Representatives, becoming the first African Americans from the South to be elected to the U.S. Congress since Reconstruction.

1977

Alex Haley's book *Roots* becomes a bestseller. The saga of his family's history begins with Kunte Kinte, an African hunter brought to the colonies as a slave.

1984

Jesse Jackson becomes a Democratic presidential candidate. He runs again in 1988.

People continue to respect the achievements of Martin Luther King Jr. and other civil rights leaders years after their deaths.

JANUARY 1986

Martin Luther King Jr.'s birthday is established as a federal holiday on the third Monday in January each year.

DECEMBER 13, 1986

Ella Baker dies at age 83.

1991

Clarence Thomas becomes the second African American appointed to the U.S. Supreme Court, filling the seat left open by Thurgood Marshall.

1992

Carol Moseley Braun is the first black woman elected to the U.S. Senate.

JANUARY 24, 1993

Thurgood Marshall dies at age 84, two years after he retired from the U.S. Supreme Court.

1994

Nelson Mandela is elected president of South Africa in the country's first election open to black voters.

Bibliography

Adler, David A. *Martin Luther King, Jr.: Free at Last.*
New York: Holiday House, 1986.

Dallard, Shyrlee. *Ella Baker: A Leader Behind the Scenes.*
Englewood Cliffs, NJ: Silver Burdett Press, 1990.

Du Bois, W.E.B. *Against Racism: Unpublished Essays,
Papers, Addresses, 1887-1961.* Amherst: University of
Massachusetts Press, 1985.

Farmer, James. *Lay Bare the Heart: An Autobiography of
the Civil Rights Movement.* New York: Arbor House,
1985.

Gardner, Carl. *Andrew Young: A Biography.* New York:
Drake, 1978.

Guinier, Lani *The Tyranny of the Majority: Fundamental
Fairness in Representative Democracy.* New York: Free
Press, 1994.

Haley, Alex. *The Autobiography of Malcolm X.* New
York: Ballantine Books, 1973.

Haskins, James. *Andrew Young: Man With a Mission.*
New York: Lothrop, Lee and Shepard, 1979.

Jakoubek, Robert E. *James Farmer and the Freedom
Rides.* Brookfield, CT: Millbrook, 1994.

King, Martin Luther, Jr. *Why We Can't Wait.* New
York: Harper and Row, 1964.

Levine, Ellen. *If You Lived at the Time of Martin Luther King*. New York: Scholastic Inc., 1990.

Lewis, David Levering. *W.E.B. Du Bois: Biography of a Race, 1868-1919*. New York: Henry Holt, 1993.

Malcolm X. *The End of White Supremacy: Four Speeches*. New York: Seaver Books, 1971.

————. *Malcolm X Talks to Young People: Speeches in the U.S., Britain, and Africa*. New York: Pathfinder Press, 1991.

————. *By Any Means Necessary*. New York: Pathfinder Press, 1992.

McKissack, Patricia. *Martin Luther King, Jr.: A Man to Remember*. Chicago: Childrens Press, 1984.

Meier, August, and Elliot Rudwick. *CORE: A Study in the Civil Rights Movement, 1942-1968*. New York: Oxford University Press, 1973.

Millender, Dharathula H. *Martin Luther King, Jr.: Boy With a Dream*. Indianapolis: Bobbs-Merrill, 1969.

Powledge, Fred. *We Shall Overcome: Heroes of the Civil Rights Movement*. New York: Scribner, 1993.

Rennert, Richard. *Civil Rights Leaders*. New York: Chelsea House, 1993.

Roberts, Naurice. *Andrew Young: Freedom Fighter*. Chicago: Childrens Press, 1983.

Rowland, Della. *Martin Luther King, Jr.: The Dream of a Peaceful Revolution.* Englewood Cliffs, NJ: Silver Burdett Press, 1990.

Salley, Columbus. *The Black 100: A Ranking of the Most Influential African-Americans, Past and Present.* Secaucus, NJ: Carol, 1994.

Sitkoff, Harvard. *The Struggle for Black Equality, 1954-1980.* New York: Hill and Wang, 1981.

Weisbrot, Robert. *Freedom Bound: A History of America's Civil Rights Movement.* New York: Norton, 1990.

Williams, Juan. *Eyes on the Prize: America's Civil Rights Years, 1954-1965.* New York: Viking Press, 1987.

Index

155

156

Muhammad, Elijah, 114, 115, 116, 119-121
Murray, Donald Gaines, 36
Muslim Mosque, Incorporated, 121

Nabrit, James Jr., 53
National Association for the Advancement of Colored People (NAACP), 23, 34, 35, 52, 64-66, 73, 100, 134; cases brought to Supreme Court by, 10, 36, 37, 38-42, 53, 100; under Du Bois leadership, 22, 24, 26-27; founding of, 22; and Montgomery bus boycott, 97
National Council of Churches, 81
National Council of Negro Women, 127
National Equal Rights Convention, 8
National Guard, 56
National Rainbow Coalition, 129
National Urban League, 100
Nation of Islam, 109, 110, 114, 116-117, 119, 121
Niagara Movement, 21-22
Nixon, E. D., 97
Nixon, Richard, 58, 85
Nkrumah, Kwame, 28, 29, 101
Nobel Peace Prize, 77, 103

nonviolent resistance, 52, 53, 54, 57, 82-83, 118; as used by Gandhi, 50, 51, 79, 95, 100, 102, 119

Operation Breadbasket, 131
Organization of Afro-American Unity (OAAU), 121

Palestine Liberation Organization (PLO), 87
Pan-African Congress, 24
Parks, Rosa, 96-97, 98
passive resistance, 79. *See also* nonviolent resistance
Peace Information Center, 27-28
People United to Save Humanity (PUSH), 131
Persian Gulf War, 131-132
Plessy v. Ferguson, 17, 36, 40
Poor People's March on Washington, 104

Ray, James Earl, 105
Reconstruction, 16, 83
Redmon, Charles Lenox, 20
Rehnquist, William, 45
Rhodesia, 71-72
riots, 104, 106
Roosevelt, Franklin D., 50, 64, 127
Rustin, Bayard, 66

158

White, Walter, 26, 27
Williams, Jenny, 92
Works Progress Administration (WPA), 64
World and Africa, The, 28
World War II, 28, 50

Young, Andrea, 81,
Young, Andrew Jackson Jr., 10; belief of, in nonviolent resistance, 79, 81; early years of, 75, 76-77; education of, 77-78; as leader of SCLC, 81, 83; as mayor of Atlanta, 87; as member of U.S. Congress, 83-85; as United Nations ambassador, 76, 85-87; work in Austria, 80; work of, with King, 76, 81-83
Young, Andrew Sr., 76, 78
Young, Andrew III, 84
Young, Daisy Fuller, 76
Young, Lisa, 81
Young, Paula, 81

Zimbabwe, 72. *See also* Rhodesia

ABOUT THE AUTHOR

KIMBERLY HAYES TAYLOR, a native of Louisville, Kentucky, is a reporter for the *Star Tribune* newspaper in Minneapolis. She writes about issues that concern young people, the poor, and people of color. Taylor, who graduated from Morehead State University in 1984, has written for the *Courier-Journal* in Louisville, the *Hartford Courant* in Connecticut, and *USA Today*. She is also the author of the forthcoming book, *Black Abolitionists and Early Freedom Fighters*.

Photo Credits